ROUTLEDGE LIBRARY EDITIONS:
HISTORY OF EDUCATION

GROWTH IN ENGLISH
EDUCATION 1946-1952

GROWTH IN ENGLISH EDUCATION

1946-1952

By

H. C. DENT

Volume 4

LONDON AND NEW YORK

First published in 1954
This edition first published in 2007 by
Routledge
2 Park Square, Milton Park, Abingdon, Oxfordshire OX14 4RN
Simultaneously published in the USA and Canada
by Routledge
711 Third Avenue, New York, NY 10017

First issued in paperback 2014

Routledge is an imprint of the Taylor & Francis Group, an informa business

Transferred to Digital Printing 2007

© 1954 Routledge

All rights reserved. No part of this book may be reprinted or reproduced or utilised in any form or by any electronic, mechanical, or other means, now known or hereafter invented, including photocopying and recording, or in any information storage or retrieval system, without permission in writing from the publishers.

British Library Cataloguing in Publication Data
A catalogue record for this book is available from the British Library

Library of Congress Cataloging in Publication Data
A catalog record for this book has been requested

ISBN 978-0-415-43216-0 (hbk)
ISBN 978-1-138-01065-9 (pbk)
ISBN 978-0-415-41978-9 (Set)

Publisher's Note
The publisher has gone to great lengths to ensure the quality of this reprint but points out that some imperfections in the original copies may be apparent.

GROWTH IN ENGLISH EDUCATION
1946–1952

by

H. C. DENT

ROUTLEDGE & KEGAN PAUL LTD
Broadway House, 68–74 Carter Lane
London

*First Published in 1954
by Routledge & Kegan Paul Ltd.,
Broadway House, 68–74 Carter Lane,
London
Printed in Great Britain
by W. & J. Mackay & Co. Ltd.,
Chatham*

'. . . measured by any criterion it seems reasonable to state that there has been more work done in the training of teachers, in the building of schools, in the making available of educational opportunity, and in the school medical service, in the three years 1945–8 than in any other three years in the history of English education.'—DR. W. P. ALEXANDER, secretary of the Association of Education Committees, writing in *Education*, January 1949.

'I claim that great as were the difficulties in 1945 to 1951 there was more progress in those six years than in any comparable six years in the history of our country.'—MISS ALICE BACON, M.P., in the House of Commons, 25th March 1952.

PREFACE

This book carries on the story of my previous volume *Education in Transition* from the passing of the Education Act, 1944, to about midway through 1952. There are, I think, good reasons for regarding those eight years as a unity, and for calling them 'Years of Expansion'. Those who, whether as teachers or administrators, were during that period actively engaged in the arduous, and often dispiriting, struggle to 'make the Act an actuality' may very naturally feel more conscious of what was not achieved than of what was. Parents of children who were then at school, and the public generally, many of whom had expected—quite irrationally—a transformation overnight, may be pardoned a sense of disappointment, even of disgruntlement. But we whose business it is to stand on the touchline and try to assess the game as a whole must acknowledge that, considering all the difficulties, what was accomplished during those few years represents an achievement to be proud of. And I think it is our bounden duty to say so.

I think it is particularly important to say so now. Britain's still precarious economic position, and the mounting claims of national defence, seem certain to slow down the rapid rate of expansion of facilities for public education which characterized the years between 1944 and 1952. As early as 1949 the first chill breezes of economy began to blow, and the Ministry of Education's Circulars 242 and 245, of December 1951 and February 1952 respectively, to my mind signalled the approaching end of an epoch. Unless there is an unexpected improvement in the international climate the next decade at least—and it is futile to try to look farther ahead—will be a time of what is euphemistically called consolidation: which means in more brutal words, of tightening one's belt and doing the best one can with diminished resources.

Because of this prospect some Jeremiahs have been moved to assure us that the 1944 Act is now dead. Nothing could be farther from the truth. Even if—as will not happen—the country never took another step towards fully implementing that Act, the impetus it gave to educational reform and the material advances it made possible during the first eight years after its passing, endowed it with a vitality which nothing short of national collapse could extinguish. These dismal prophets stand convicted of a double failure in understanding; they have failed to distinguish between reorganization and re-equipment of the educational system and reform in education, and they have further failed to appreciate that so long as the increased momentum which has been given to the latter persists so long will the purposes of the Act continue to be fulfilled, however little material progress may be taking place.

What matters above all to our country is the extent and, even more, the quality of the educational *reform* set in motion by the passing of the 1944 Act. Reorganization and re-equipment are but means to that end. It is true that as late as 1952 two of the more important items in the projected reorganization, the raising of the school leaving age to 16 and the introduction of universal compulsory part-time education up to the age of 18, had not been reached, and were indeed not in sight. It is true also that many classes were still too large and that there were still thousands of out-of-date and ill-equipped school buildings. In short, both reorganization and re-equipment were still far from complete. But even if by some miracle both had been completed, that would have been no guarantee that any educational reform had taken place. The two are not necessarily connected;

when they are, it is as a rule reform which compels reorganization, not vice versa. What is, I think, the most encouraging feature of the eight years surveyed in this book is the fact that the two processes went hand in hand together, each stimulating and aiding the other. The difficulty in the years ahead will be to prevent the (I fear inevitable) slowing down of re-equipment from so discouraging teachers and administrators that they will slacken in their efforts for reform. I hope the following pages may offer them some little encouragement to persist.

I have not attempted here anything in the way of a systematic history. I have simply tried to show something of what has been done—and not done—in various broad fields of public education, treating each of these fields separately so as to give, I hope, a clearer picture. If this does no more, I hope it may at least give some idea of the way in which this country, maimed by war, has set out to recover its strength, for what it has attempted in education is paralleled by what it has tried to do in other areas of the national life.

On occasions I have allowed myself the luxury of comment; on all such it is my own personal opinion which is expressed, and not that of any body with which I am or have been connected.

I wish to express my gratitude to Professor W. J. H. Sprott, editor of the International Library of Sociology and Social Reconstruction, for some most helpful criticisms.

London, August 1953
H. C. DENT

CONTENTS

PREFACE	*page* ix
I. EMERGENCY MEASURES	1
II. PERMANENT STRUCTURE	30
III. EXPERIMENT IN SECONDARY EDUCATION	67
IV. OPPORTUNITIES FOR ADULTS	130
V. UNIVERSITY EXPANSION	164
INDEX	203

Chapter One

EMERGENCY MEASURES

THE EDUCATION ACT, 1944, faced those who had to administer it with a multitude of problems and a mass of work. Some of the latter had to be begun at once and done very quickly, for the bulk of the Act was due to come into operation on 1st April 1945, less than seven months after its passing in early August 1944.

It is worth recalling that in August 1944 not only was the war still at its height but that the country was being subjected to incessant attack by 'flying' bombs which, in addition to causing widespread damage, especially in the London area, had re-started evacuation on a large scale. Between the beginning of July and the first week in August over 200,000 children, most of them of school age, poured out of London into the areas of scores of other authorities. It was in such circumstances that the Ministry and the local education authorities set to work to 'convert legal phraseology into a living force', as Mr. Butler put it in Circular 1.[1]

This circular, in addition to prescribing immediate tasks for the local authorities, warned also of others quickly to follow: notably of the comprehensive surveys of their areas and the Development Plans elaborating complete and detailed schemes for providing primary and secondary education which the authorities were required by the Act to make. But at least it

[1] Ministry of Education Circular No. 1. *The Education Act, 1944.* Dated 15th August 1944. H.M. Stationery Office.

relieved the minds of the authorities of their overriding anxiety. The school leaving age, it said, would not be raised on 1st April 1945, nor in all probability within one year thereafter.

The decision to delay the raising of compulsory school age was widely and strongly criticized at the time. But no other decision would have been practicable. There were neither buildings nor teachers available for the children who would have been retained in school. It might conceivably have been possible to house the 14-year-olds in some sort of fashion by pressing into service all kinds of improvised accommodation —though the failure of the continuation school clauses of the 1918 Act warned against such an expedient—but by no imaginable means could a sufficient body of teachers have been got together at that date. In fact, the project which was to produce them was only just beginning to get under way.

How to provide the additional teachers which the 1944 Act would demand was a problem which early began to exercise minds at the Ministry and elsewhere. It had two facets: recruitment and training, of which the latter was much the more formidable. Men and women ready to try their hands at teaching are usually not difficult to secure in fair numbers, provided that little or no regard be paid to qualifications. But everyone concerned with bringing the 1944 Act into operation was resolutely determined to ensure that its reforms should be launched only by fully qualified, which meant trained, teachers. Yet the more they looked at the existing facilities for training teachers the less adequate these appeared to produce within any reasonable period anything like the very large number of teachers which would be needed.

Before the war the training colleges and the university training departments were together producing fewer than 7,000 trained teachers a year. It was conservatively estimated that to replace war casualties and cover the raising of the school age 70,000 additional teachers would be required. A simple arithmetical calculation showed that even supposing the normal training facilities could at once be doubled after the war—a most improbable contingency—it would still take ten years to make up the necessary numbers. And so, at some time during 1943, there was born the 'exciting but dangerous' idea of a special scheme of emergency training, self-contained in its own colleges, offering courses shorter but more intensive than the normal ones to men and women of rather more mature years than the average student entering training college or university training department.

'INTO THE BREACH'

There appears to be some doubt as to who first suggested the idea of the Emergency Training Scheme for Teachers. It may be, as has been claimed, that it originated within the National Union of Teachers. Or that someone in the Board of Education conceived it. Or that, as so often happens with original ideas, it occurred to several people almost simultaneously. At this date the point is academic. In any case the idea was not completely novel, for emergency measures had been taken to increase the teaching force after the 1914–18 war. The features which made this scheme distinctive were its breadth of conception, its flexibility and the thoroughness of its detailed planning. That the machinery devised for its execution broke down rather badly at times was due, not so much to faulty staff work, as was widely believed at the time, as to a succession of circumstances over which those who designed it had little or no control; and not least to the amazingly large and enthusiastic response it received.

During the latter half of 1943 preliminary discussions about the proposed scheme took place between the Board of Education and representatives of the local education authorities, the teachers, and the training colleges. These were followed by meetings held all over the country to enable the Board to obtain a complete cross-section of professional opinion. This was at first by no means entirely favourable; there were many doubts and fears to be overcome, especially among the teachers.

That was not at all surprising. The English elementary school teacher had had a long, stern struggle (which, it may be added, has not even yet been brought to an entirely satisfactory conclusion) to achieve something like due recognition of his professional status, and his representatives would have been much more (or less) than human had they not looked with exceedingly wary eyes at a scheme which could so easily threaten that hard-won status. 'The consequences of a rather large scale measure of dilution of the teaching profession cannot be ignored', wrote the National Union of Teachers.[1] Others expressed themselves in starker terms; the scheme, they said, would 'flood the profession with half-trained teachers'. Some even said 'half-baked'.

To give the teachers due credit, they were concerned not only for their own status but also for the children in the schools. They were fearful lest these should suffer from being taught by inadequately equipped teachers. And they had a thought, too, for the men and women who might enter teaching by way of an emergency scheme; they saw the possibility that, starting with lower academic qualifications and receiving a shorter training, these might be regarded as an inferior grade of the profession, condemned throughout their careers to remain in its lower ranks.

Gradually, however, the hard facts of the situation forced themselves home; only by extraordinary measures could sufficient teachers be produced to carry through reforms which the entire teaching profession desired, which indeed it had been largely instrumental in placing on the Statute Book. By October 1943 sufficient agreement had been reached to enable Mr. Butler to tell the House of Commons briefly what was proposed. In December he appointed a departmental committee, representative of the Board of Education, H.M. Inspec-

[1] In *A Short Term Policy for an Emergency*, October 1943, p. 10.

torate, the local education authorities, the teachers and the training establishments, under the chairmanship of Mr. G. N. Flemming, a senior officer of the Board,[1] to study the problems involved and advise upon a course of action.

This committee's report was published in May 1944. With it was an introductory circular[2] which stated that the Board proposed to take its recommendations as a basis for action. A week later advertisements appeared in the Press for teachers willing to serve in the colleges to be set up to give emergency training. Thus was launched what was probably the most daring large-scale experiment ever made in the history of English education. Had it not been essayed, or had it failed, there would have been, in fact, no Education Act, 1944; that measure would have remained a 'scrap of paper'. Happily, it was essayed, and it did not fail.

In brief, what the Flemming Committee proposed was that men and women, between approximately the ages of 21 and 35, who had served in H.M. Forces or engaged in other forms of national service for at least twelve months during the war should be invited to apply for a one-year course of training, followed by two years of part-time study while teaching, on the successful completion of which they would be recognized as fully qualified teachers. The academic qualifications normally required for entry to a teacher training college would not be insisted upon, though candidates would be expected to give evidence of 'a sufficient background of general education and culture to enable them to become worthy members of the profession'. Personal qualities were to be taken very seriously into account; this was no scheme to recruit 'stopgaps', but was intended to enrich as well as enlarge the teaching profession. The training would be carried out in colleges specially created,

---

[1] Now Sir Gilbert Flemming, Permanent Secretary of the Ministry of Education.

[2] Board of Education Circular 1652. *Emergency Recruitment and Training of Teachers*, dated 15th May 1944. H.M. Stationery Office.

staffed, and equipped for the purpose; it would be free, and students would be given maintenance grants to support themselves and their dependants.

With a prudence which does not always characterize English experiments the Board of Education decided to try out the scheme first on a small scale. In September 1944 a group of twenty-seven men and one woman assembled at Nottingham University College[1] to take a 'pilot' course under the direction of the principal and staff of Goldsmiths' College, University of London, then in evacuation quarters at Nottingham.

It is credibly reported that so impressed were these students with the idea that theirs was to be an *intensive* course that none of them brought any sports gear or clothing. They were quickly persuaded out of that unwisdom, but work intensively they certainly did—and thoroughly enjoyed the experience, as did also their tutors. The course was a great success, and many valuable lessons were learned.[2] A second course of the same kind was run by Goldsmiths' during the following year.

Before the end of 1944 it had become clear which way the war was going, and so in December applications for training under the Emergency Scheme were invited from men and women released from H.M. Forces on medical grounds, men in medical grades III and IV, and women in civilian employment rated as war service, this last being interpreted so broadly as to exclude few applicants. From the start applications came in great numbers. By March 1945 over 7,000 had been received, and when, following the end of the war in Europe, in June the invitation to apply was thrown open to all men and women in the Forces and war industries the rate doubled and redoubled almost week by week. By December it had risen to 5,000 a month, and even this was exceeded in the early months of 1946, a peak of 6,000 being reached in March.

[1] Now the University of Nottingham.
[2] For a detailed account of the Nottingham experiment see *Teachers from the Forces*, edited by Dr. M. M. Lewis, the director of the courses. Harrap, 1946.

The Ministry of Education's plans were seriously disrupted by the sudden end of the war in Japan. It seems, too, that even in their most optimistic moments its officers had not anticipated anything like so large a number of applications as was received. Throughout the second half of 1945 and the whole of 1946 despite the strenuous efforts of numerous interviewing panels at home and overseas the acceptance of candidates for training lagged terribly behind the torrent of applications. The entry of accepted candidates into college lagged even worse; by the middle of 1946 there was a waiting list of 25,000, and some 7,500 more, unable to stand the delay, had withdrawn. It was not until March 1947 that the colleges began to catch up. Many candidates, chiefly among the men, had to wait a year, eighteen months, or even two years between acceptance and entry into college. Local education authorities, at the urgent request of the Ministry, found jobs for thousands as temporary teachers, or as clerks in their offices, and so tided them over the period of waiting. But other thousands of potentially good teachers were undoubtedly lost to the country through these unhappy delays.

The Ministry of Education was overwhelmed with abuse from all sides. Some of it was perhaps deserved; it may be that in the early days the Ministry, which was not designed to be an executive body, tried to do too much off its own bat, and did not sufficiently enlist the aid of those experienced and indefatigable improvisors, the local education authorities. But most of it was not. Like everyone else, the Ministry had expected the war in the Far East to last much longer than it did. Like everyone else, its officers had been led to believe that in any case demobilization, unlike that after World War I, would be reasonably gradual. As it was, Japan collapsed suddenly, demobilization was rapid, the Emergency Training Scheme was popular beyond all imagining, and the quality of the applicants exceeded expectations. Hence a flow of applications which snowed under the Ministry's clerical staff, and a mounting host of accepted candidates for whom there were no colleges.

Had the initial assumptions held good the provision of colleges would have been considered reasonably rapid. The first three were opened in May and June 1945: at Wall Hall near Watford, Exhall near Coventry, and Alnwick in Northumberland. By December 1945 six were working, and by the following December, thirty-one. This was, in fact, no slight achievement, but it seemed at the time a shockingly slow progress, and many of us had no hesitation in telling the Ministry so. Now that we know the circumstances more fully it is only right to make something in the way of an *amende honorable*.

To find and equip at short notice some fifty sets of premises suitable to accommodate residential colleges—establishments which require rather exceptional specialized accommodation—would have been at the best of times a difficult task. Between 1944 and 1947 was the worst of times. Most properties likely to be suitable had been requisitioned during the war by Government departments or business firms, few of which showed much disposition to surrender them. The Ministry of Education was far from being the only body on the search for accommodation; in particular, troops were returning home from oversea in large numbers, and premises for use as temporary barracks were greatly in demand. And when a place which seemed possible had been tracked down and secured shortages of labour and materials rendered its rapid adaptation and equipment virtually impossible.

Those numerous and vociferous critics who incessantly told the Ministry of the multitude of 'large country houses' that were to be had for the asking (if only, they said, the Ministry had the energy to look for them) had no idea how few such houses exist, how ill-suited are the rooms of most of them for college purposes, and how inadequate their plumbing systems to cope with large numbers. Bitter experience, the result of many fruitless journeys, convinced the Ministry that the 'large country house', far from being the complete and easy answer to the problem, was 'seldom practicable and never wholly satisfactory'.[1] Of the fifty-five emergency colleges ultimately established, only five found homes in country mansions,[2] and the accommodation provided by two of these had to be supplemented by hutting.

Far more students, indeed, did their training in huts than in baronial halls; fifteen of the colleges were accommodated in industrial hostels, five in hutted hospitals, three in army camps, and five in other kinds of temporary buildings. Among the variety of buildings used were a former theological college, an elementary school, an orphanage, and a home for destitute persons.

The students ranged widely in age and came from almost every social and vocational background. Although the Ministry of Education, in Circular 18 (19th December 1944), had specified that the age limits should normally be 21 to 35, the latter limit was frequently exceeded; well over 1,000 students were on acceptance aged 40 or more. On the other hand, very few candidates under the age of 21 were accepted; they were advised to take the normal two-year course of training. To give an idea of the range of previous occupations, in one men's college of 216 students thirty-eight were represented, in a women's college of 179 students twenty-four. This was typical; but by far the largest proportion of students came from commercial or clerical employments; if those from the civil and local government services be included, they made up well over half. About one-sixth came from industry. Of all students, fewer than one in twelve had had any previous teaching experience.

It was popularly believed at the time that most of the students had had only an elementary school education, and had

---

[1] *Challenge and Response. An Account of the Emergency Scheme for the Training of Teachers.* Ministry of Education Pamphlet No. 17. H.M. Stationery Office, 1950, p. 16. This gives a detailed and vivid account of the Scheme.

[2] Alnwick Castle, Wall Hall, Newland Park (Bucks), Trent Park (Herts), and Wynyard Hall (Durham).

left school at the age of 14 or shortly afterwards. This was far from being the case. Over three-quarters of those who entered college had attended a secondary or technical school, and of these nearly two-thirds possessed a School Certificate or some higher examination certificate. Nearly 1,000 had the Higher School Certificate, and over 200 university degrees. Many others had pursued systematic courses of study or reading after leaving school.

'From the educational point of view, the most significant feature of the emergency training scheme was the actual quality of the students themselves. Three characteristics stood out: their keenness, and singleness of purpose; the wide range of their talents and accomplishments; and their powers of initiative and organization.' Thus the Ministry of Education's official account of the Emergency Training Scheme.[1] Government reports on governmental enterprises can hardly expect to escape the suspicion that they are looking at their work through rose-tinted spectacles; but in this case the official judgement is supported by everyone who had to do with the scheme—at least during its earlier stages. These characteristics were not so universal later.

An outside observer who visited many of the colleges has written:[2]

'The personal quality of the students, too, varied enormously; but there were, as constant factors, the richness and diversity of experience and background which provided the necessary climatic conditions for that "cross-fertilization of theory and experience" regarded by Sir Richard Livingstone as so essential to a fully developed being.'

The staffing of the colleges was perhaps the most daring feature of the whole experiment. Nearly 90 per cent of the principals and assistant staff were teachers from primary and secondary schools. Of 1,211 who were serving in September

[1] *Challenge and Response*, p. 36.
[2] Miss Loveday Martin, in *Into the Breach*. Turnstile Press, 1949, p. 14.

EMERGENCY MEASURES

1948 only sixty had come from training colleges. Grammar schools had contributed twenty principals and 557 lecturers, modern schools eight principals and 306 lecturers, and primary schools one principal and 171 lecturers. Eleven principals and seventy-seven lecturers had been drawn from the ranks of local inspectors and organizers, and teachers in technical colleges. Most of the 1,211 had come direct from their schools, the main exception being that about one-quarter of the men lecturers had had an intervening period in the Forces.

There is no doubt that this use of serving teachers proved a resounding success. The Ministry of Education, in *Challenge and Response*, declared that it was 'one of the principal strengths of the emergency training staffs that they came fresh from the teaching of children'.[1] It is only fair to add, as the Ministry did, that the break with classroom experience provided by service in the Forces also proved of great value, for the obvious reason that 'lecturers with Service experience had sympathy with the point of view of ex-Service men and women'.[2] As over five-sixths of the men students and over a quarter of the women came from the Services this point needs no emphasis.

A word of tribute should be paid to the local education authorities and the managers and governors of voluntary schools who responded so readily to the Ministry's request that they would release teachers for service on the staffs of emergency colleges. They had to give up some of their best teachers at a time when not only was there an absolute shortage of teachers, but the profession lacked most of its younger and more virile members. Yet rarely was there a case of refusal or even unwillingness, though clearly there was grave risk involved in taking teaching strength from schools which were still in the throes of recovery from the manifold evil effects of war-time conditions.

The Flemming Committee had suggested in their report

[1] p. 55. [2] p. 54.

that the one year's training for emergency students should be arranged somewhat as follows:

Preparatory Stage, including school visits	6 weeks
Main Course, Part I	4 weeks
Teaching Practice	3 weeks
Vacation	1 week
Main Course, Part II	12 weeks
Vacation	2 weeks
Teaching Practice	9 weeks
Vacation	1 week
Main Course, Part III	14 weeks
	52 weeks

Every college modified this plan. Most found the 'preparatory stage' too long: if they were in any doubt about this the students usually enlightened them! Often it was cut to three weeks, and in some cases to two. In the time thus saved many colleges gave a general course during which students could decide whether they wished to train for primary or secondary work. Almost all the colleges gave their students three periods of teaching practice instead of two. But the really substantial change, made in January 1946, was the lengthening of the course from twelve to thirteen months. The necessity for this was an index of its intensiveness. Under the revised arrangement the total working period became forty-eight weeks, allowance being made for from four to eight weeks' vacation during the session and up to eight weeks on its conclusion. This last was undoubtedly a wise provision; during the earlier days there were frequent cases of students completing their training on a Friday and taking up a teaching post on the following Monday: which could have been good neither for themselves nor the children they had to teach.

As the colleges adapted the layout of the course to suit their particular circumstances, so they took liberties with the suggestions about the curriculum made in the Flemming Report. The varieties of curriculum and method were indeed innumerable; it is not enough to say that each college had its own, for often a college would change either or both from year to year, and even within a year's course. Principals and lecturers were ever on the look-out for ways in which to improve their techniques; and it is probable that never before in the history of teacher training did the student body so impose its ideas upon the teaching staff. The instance quoted in *Challenge and Response*[1] of the interviewing panel which advised that: 'Mr. X should be posted to a college with a strong Principal and staff, or he will run the place' could have been multiplied many times. But it was not only, nor largely, because of the presence of dominating personalities among the students that curricula and methods were so particularly 'student-centred'; it was chiefly because the maturity of outlook and variety of adult experience so commonly to be found enabled the students to offer many valuable suggestions for their better training.

Nevertheless, despite infinite variety in detail, the courses all subserved the four guiding principles laid down by the Flemming Committee. These were: first, that 'students must be given full opportunities of studying and practising educational methods and techniques'; second, that they should be afforded 'every possible facility for reading and thinking about education in the wider sense, having regard to its individual, social and ethical implications, and to its setting in the general pattern of life'; third, that every student should take 'a course designed to ensure competent use of the English language'; and fourth, that everyone should make a close study of a field or fields of knowledge chosen because of its (or their) intrinsic interest *for the student as a person*. This last principle, affirmed long previously by the Departmental Committee on the Training of Teachers which reported in 1925, was first introduced into practice on a

[1] p. 25.

EMERGENCY MEASURES

large scale during the Emergency Training Scheme. Its benefits were so obvious that it was everywhere adopted by the Institutes of Education set up in 1947–8.

Only three subjects were made compulsory for all students: the principles and practice of education, health education, and English usage. Beyond these students were free to choose, in consultation with their tutors, whatever subject or combination of subjects they preferred. It is fair to say that in the great majority of cases this freedom was wisely exercised, and that the colleges did their utmost to provide courses which 'reflected the individual needs of the students, the requirements of the schools, the talents of the staff, and the opportunities provided by the environment and circumstances of the college'.[1]

It is impossible to give in short space any adequate idea of the wide variety of teaching methods employed during the six years the scheme was in operation. But there are, I think, three keys to understanding why unconventional and heterodox methods were often used—in some cases, actually invented. First, the maturity of the students, which demanded a very different approach from that suitable for the 18-year-olds who normally enter training college. This was particularly noticeable when, as happened in some colleges towards the end of the scheme, emergency and two-year students were under the same roof. 'They are such children', said one emergency student, who was herself but a year or two older than the 'infants' she was commenting on. But she had been in the Services, where intelligent young people grow up fast, especially in war-time.

Second, very many of the emergency students—perhaps in the earlier days most of them—had applied for training because they felt a strong urge to take up teaching as a means of rendering social service. They were consequently deeply interested in the sociological aspects of education. Third, as has been mentioned, a very large proportion of the teaching staff was

[1] *Challenge and Response*, p. 65.

recruited direct from primary and secondary schools, and they brought with them their own methods, which were by no means always those of the training college. Moreover, throughout the duration of the scheme the Ministry of Education, both directly and through H.M. Inspectors, gave every encouragement to the colleges to experiment freely with curricula and methods. Many took the fullest advantage of the freedom thus offered.

It will then be readily understood why formal lectures bulked much less largely than in the normal training colleges, and why discussions and seminars played a much more prominent part; why investigation of the sociological background of the school assumed an importance hitherto rarely found in teacher training; and why the students did so much more practical work than had previously been customary. Large-scale projects, for example, were a feature at many colleges, but not necessarily nor even usually with the primary aim of sending out teachers to teach by the 'project' method. What methods a student would later use was considered a matter for personal decision. In college he or she did projects for quite other purposes: for self-education, and in order to learn by personal experience the difficulties which confront children set to similar work. The same motive inspired much of the practical work in art, crafts and music undertaken by students.

One of the most remarkable outcomes of the Emergency Scheme was the astonishing amount of latent talent which it uncovered. 'I had no idea I could do that!' was one of the most common observations to be heard in the colleges: and 'that' might be anything from writing a poem to constructing a switchboard or from painting a landscape to chairing a committee. One might almost say that the scheme was justified by the unsuspected capacity it released in those who underwent training.

The most controversial feature of the training programme was beyond doubt the procedure adopted for assessing the fitness of a student to become a teacher. About this point the Flemming Committee had written:

'We consider that a formal *external* examination of the usual type would not be desirable, as being bound to go too far in restricting the freedom of the college staff in planning suitable courses . . . would exert additional pressure of an undesirable kind on students . . . [and demand] elaborate machinery . . . quite inappropriate to a temporary scheme . . . We recommend, therefore, that the work of the students should be assessed on the basis of internal tests for which the staff of the college would be responsible. Internal tests must, however, be subject to a fully effective external check and the Board of Education must be in a position to take responsibility for the maintenance of a national standard. Full records must be kept in such a form that an external assessor can see how assessments are being made. The process of testing and recording should be continuous and the external assessor should have the opportunity of being associated with the process at all stages, and not merely at the end of the course.'

I have quoted this passage at length because not only at the time but also later there were misunderstandings and misgivings about the value of a qualification based on 'assessment'. Many teachers regarded—and some still regard—assessment as a less rigorous form of testing than examination. As late as August 1951 the Professor of Education at Manchester University declared his belief[1] that no other profession admitted entrants on such easy terms. This despite the fact that for thirty years there had been no final written or practical examinations in the Education Department at Bristol University, where from the start the work of the students had been assessed continuously by internal examination and other tests throughout the session.

There were—and are—good reasons for the fears expressed

[1] Professor R. A. C. Oliver, in the *Universities Quarterly*. Article on 'Institutes of Education'.

about assessment as a substitute for examination. Casually or inadequately conducted, assessment must lead to a lowering of standards and may lead to intolerable abuses. But when the system of 'cumulative assessment', as it is called, that is, continuous assessment resulting in the building up of a cumulative record of the student's work, progress, interests and personality development, is conscientiously and thoroughly carried out, assessment constitutes a far more searching test than any battery of formal examinations at the end of a course. Many of the emergency-trained students were uncomfortably aware of this. Cases were recorded of petitions to principals to restore the examination system; because, said the petitioners, they felt that they were for ever being followed about and watched and marked.

All teachers trained under the Emergency Scheme had to serve two years on probation—twice as long as teachers who have had a normal course of training—and during these two years they were expected to follow a systematic course of part-time study. The Flemming Committee had suggested that these courses should be drafted by the students in consultation with their college tutors and approved by the Ministry of Education, but in Circular 106 (22nd May 1946) the Ministry virtually handed the task over to the local education authorities. Thereafter the amount and quality of the study done by emergency-trained teachers depended partly, at least, on the facilities provided for them by their authorities. Left to their own resources, as unfortunately they were in some areas, many of them were inclined to find, as one put it, that 'the trouble with part-time study is that there is no part-time'.

Many authorities took the task very seriously. Some appointed an officer to be 'guide, philosopher and friend' to all emergency-trained teachers in the area. Others placed groups of probationers in the care of selected head teachers. Many drew up courses of study and reading lists, and quite a few gathered their probationers together periodically for week-end or longer

EMERGENCY MEASURES

residential courses, which were greatly appreciated. A number of the emergency colleges did the same, and these gatherings, which frequently took the form of annual reunions, were perhaps even more valuable, for they encouraged a frankness of comment which many newly-fledged teachers hardly dared to permit themselves in the presence of their employers!

The Emergency Training Scheme came to a close in October 1951, when the last group of students passed out of Trent Park College in Hertfordshire. It produced altogether some 35,000 qualified teachers—more than 23,000 men and nearly 12,000 women—which means that by the end of that year about one teacher in six serving in maintained primary and secondary schools had come from an emergency college. It is too early yet to offer any opinion about the ultimate success of the scheme; only when those emergency-trained teachers who have remained in the profession have been teaching for ten, fifteen or twenty years will it be possible fully to assess that. Meanwhile, what can, and should, be said is that a daring experiment, boldly conceived and, all things considered, admirably carried out, enabled great educational reforms to be set in motion and sustained which otherwise could not have been launched.

But I think that something more than that should be said. On my fairly frequent visits to schools during recent years I have made a point of asking the Heads' opinions about the emergency-trained teachers on their staffs. I have rarely received any but a good report, and many Heads have been enthusiastic. There can be little doubt that the profession has been enriched by many men and women who, whatever their other qualifications, have started their teaching careers 'with a refreshing sense of the adventure of teaching and a lively awareness of the new paths of learning and discovery that have been opening up before them'.[1] When during the summer term of 1952 I made an intensive sample survey of secondary

[1] *Challenge and Response*, p. 119.

modern schools which carried me into the areas of a dozen local education authorities several Heads went out of their way to tell me, without my asking, what excellent work some of their emergency-trained teachers were doing, and in particular what marked initiative they were showing. It was not unusual to find an emergency-trained teacher occupying a key post in a modern school, especially on the arts and crafts side. And already a few emergency-trained teachers had been appointed Heads of schools. It will be extraordinarily interesting to watch their progress through the years.

HORSA AND SFORSA

Not only teachers but also accommodation was needed to enable compulsory school age to be raised on 1st April 1947. That sufficient school places were made available in time was due to the successful carrying through of an emergency building scheme which, though less spectacular, was in its way as great a triumph as the Emergency Training Scheme for Teachers. Those teachers who had to wait so long for the arrival of HORSA[1] huts, and then, as so often happened, wait again because of hold-ups in their construction, and equipment with SFORSA[2] furniture, may be pardoned if they take a somewhat less enthusiastic view of this project than I do; but, as I said in my preface, those on the touchline can sometimes assess a game more objectively than the players.

The beginnings of the scheme were not auspicious. In Circular 48 (24th May 1945) the Minister of Education informed local education authorities that the allocation of building labour and materials for schools for the following twelve months 'will not suffice to do more than meet the most immediate and pressing needs, and even so only by means of improvisation and emergency provision'. First among 'the

[1] Hutting Operation for the Raising of the School Age.
[2] School Furniture Operation for the Raising of the School Age.

most immediate tasks' was placed 'the provision of such additional school accommodation as may be needed to enable the compulsory school age to be raised to 15'. The circular stated that for the time being it would not be generally possible to undertake permanent building; 'the provision of new additional accommodation must continue . . . to be made mainly in the form of prefabricated huts, which may be erected quickly with a minimum of skilled labour'. Accordingly, authorities were asked to submit 'estimates of their minimum essential requirements for school accommodation sufficient to provide for the extra age group (14–15) on a classroom basis, framed in terms of class spaces for new construction (i.e., of prefabricated huts) and of cost in respect of repairs to damaged schools'.

Four months later the new Minister of Education, Miss Ellen Wilkinson, who succeeded Mr. R. A. Butler on the return of a Labour Government in July 1945, told local education authorities in Circular 64 (27th September 1945) that after having surveyed all the demands that would be made upon building labour and materials by the educational services she had concluded that compulsory school age could not be raised before 1st April 1947. Moreover, she said:

'It is clear that the amount of new building required . . . can only be completed if a very early start is made, and if the work is spread over the period up to September 1948, when the full extra group will be in the schools . . . even so . . . the accommodation cannot be provided in time unless every means is adopted for accelerating the planning and provision and for eliminating so far as possible the need for official sanctions.'

Consequently, Miss Wilkinson said, she had made arrangements whereby the Ministry of Works would, on request, provide and erect for local education authorities any prefabricated huts they required for accommodating the extra age group. She hoped that all authorities would avail themselves of this service. The Ministry of Works would do the entire job for an annual payment of 8 per cent of the total cost of each hut and the work of erecting it, including preparation of the site. The annual payment would be recognized for grant, and would cease to be payable as soon as a hut went out of use.

The huts offered were of two standardized types, one being 24 ft. wide and the other 18 ft. 6 in. (The latter type was soon found to have grave disadvantages and was finally discarded.) Their walls were made of reinforced concrete frames having a span of 6 ft. from centre to centre. The floor was of concrete finished with wood-filled pitch mastic, and the roof of corrugated asbestos sheeting screwed on to timber purlins spanning between the concrete frames of the walls. Standard metal windows were fitted into the upper panels of the wall frames, and the remainder of the wall space was filled with 4-in. hollow blocks externally waterproofed and internally distempered, or similarly treated. Internal partitions were of 4-in. hollow blocks or 4½-in. brickwork. Lighting was normally by electricity, heating by hot water system if lavatory accommodation was included but otherwise by slow combustion stove.

The huts were normally to be erected in school playgrounds or on other land already owned by the authority, or in the case of voluntary schools by the managers or governors. A time schedule for their erection was proposed[1] whereby one-fifth of the huts required would be erected before 31st August 1946, two-fifths between that date and 31st August 1947, and the remaining two-fifths in the year ending 31st August 1948.

It will be seen from the foregoing description that the HORSA huts were by no means flimsy structures; and the general opinion of those who have had to use them over a period of years is that they are reasonably comfortable, well-lighted, heated and ventilated, and in many respects much superior to most of the permanent buildings they supplemented, though

[1] In Administrative Memorandum (A.M.) 98 (23rd October 1945), from which the details of their structure are taken.

perhaps rather too prone to require minor repairs. But when they were first offered all sorts of objections to them were raised.

Some authorities rather resented the fact that the Ministry had taken the initiative; they felt that this cast a slur upon their efficiency by suggesting that a central department could supply and erect buildings faster and better than they could themselves. But many more feared that these proposed huts would spread a dreary rash of uniformly dull structures across the country. This fear was not without cause; their warmest supporters can hardly claim that HORSA huts embellish the landscape, though many have fitted into it better than was generally expected, and some schools have done wonders by planting creepers, rambler roses or other climbing plants, or by tasteful use of colour in external decoration.

Many authorities objected strongly to the idea of occupying already exiguous playground or playing field space with buildings. Again, they had reason; not until very recent years have English schools been provided with anything like sufficient outdoor space. Many, perhaps most, of the authorities were also extremely dissatisfied with the financial terms upon which the huts were offered. They needed no reminding that 'temporary' buildings—in most cases unsightly wooden huts—erected shortly after World War I were still being used as school premises, and they saw themselves committed to paying 8 per cent for an indefinite number of years. They pointed out with some vigour that in twelve and a half years they would have paid for the total cost of a hut and its erection, and asked for assurances that if any huts were still in use after that period they would not have to continue paying rent for them.

Because of these doubts and misgivings there was for some time considerable reluctance to take up the Minister's offer, despite the fact that in Circular 64 the authorities had been told that there was very little chance of getting buildings by other means. The London County Council accepted promptly, but other authorities hung back or made alternative proposals. Essex were not satisfied that the Ministry of Works huts were the only solution to the problem, and suggested light construction permanent building. Flintshire asked permission to build 'austerity' schools. Somerset decided to supply and erect its own huts. And so on.

Doubting Thomases were encouraged to persist in their attitude by a memorandum which the Royal Institute of British Architects issued early in 1946. This disapproved strongly of these 'army-type huts', which it declared would be 'inconvenient in use, sub-standard in accommodation, uneconomical to heat, erected on playing space, and unnecessarily costly'. The R.I.B.A. recommended instead a system of construction using standardized steel frames with temporary or permanent cladding.

So small was the response to her offer that in April 1946 the Minister was moved, in A.M. 142 (9th April 1946), to express great concern 'at the very slow rate at which the Forms S.B.5 [containing particulars of huts required] are being put forward to the Ministry of Works', and pointed out that 'the difficulties of the building industry at the present time are such that the hut programme will be seriously endangered unless the demand for labour and materials can be spread over the period available'.

Gradually the stern realities of the situation impressed themselves upon the authorities' minds. The building of permanent schools on any considerable scale, they realized, was for the time being out of the question; neither labour nor materials could be got. The Government was in fact about to take the decision—which up to 1952 had not been rescinded—to restrict new school building to three categories: replacement of premises destroyed by enemy action, provision of schools for new housing estates, and provision of school places to make room for the progressively larger numbers of young children who would enter the schools from 1947 onwards owing to the increase of the birth rate from about 1942.

By mid-1946 it had become clear to the authorities that the only alternatives to HORSA huts were premises designed for other purposes, such as church halls, and surplus war-time huts. Suitable premises that could be hired were rare, especially in areas most needing additional accommodation, and surplus huts, the authorities discovered, usually cost more time, money and labour to dismantle and re-erect than new building, and even so were as a rule extremely unsatisfactory. Meanwhile the Ministry of Works was undoubtedly ready and able to supply and erect whatever huts were required, though, it must be added, in many cases only after exasperating delays: which may or may not have been the Ministry's fault.

One after one the doubters came in. Essex, for example, in May 1946 applied for 142 classrooms and ninety-four practical work rooms. By August Miss Wilkinson could tell the House of Commons that only three authorities had not submitted hutting programmes. Thirteen had stated that they needed no huts, and one was using a special type made locally. By the end of the year contracts had been placed for 1,155 classrooms and 373 practical work rooms.

Contracts placed did not necessarily mean, however, that huts would spring into position overnight. On the contrary, right to the very end of this emergency building scheme there was widespread doubt, which found expression in incessant Parliamentary questions and Press comments, whether the number of huts ready for occupation would keep pace with the growing number of 14-year-old children retained at school. It was not only the erection of the huts which was in question but also their equipment; there were often cases where huts stood ready for weeks waiting for fitments or furniture.

As early as 1944 the Ministry of Education had begun to look into the possibility of providing standardized furniture to go with the standardized huts. In July of that year, in conjunction with the Ministry of Works, it set up a school furniture and equipment sub-committee. This committee did not report until November 1946, but long before that the Ministry had made the first moves towards equipping the HORSA huts.

Early in 1946 the local education authorities were asked, in A.M. 125 (18th February 1946), to review their existing stocks of school furniture, estimate their additional requirements, and submit particulars of the latter to the Ministry. Their demands were to be restricted to the absolute minimum; only some half-dozen essential items—chairs, tables, benches, cupboards, bookshelves and blackboards—were to be asked for. School furniture, like domestic furniture, was at the time in very short supply. It was not until a full year later that the Ministry was able to offer to the authorities (in A.M. 210, 17th February 1947) a complete range of SFORSA furniture. But there was this to be said for the delay; when the furniture came, it was good. I have seen none better except hand-made 'luxury' products, the loving work of individual craftsmen, which are unfortunately beyond the purses of the maintained schools. And once the flow of supplies started it was abundant; by the end of 1948 more than a quarter of a million chairs and nearly as many desks—to mention but two items—had been issued to the schools.

Like so many feats of improvisation during these difficult days, the HORSA and SFORSA scheme did not quite succeed in scrambling home on time. It ought to have been completed by September 1948; actually, at the end of that year there were still over 1,000 rooms in process of being constructed or equipped. But 3,583 classrooms and 1,629 work rooms had been completed. Altogether the Ministry of Works provided the schools with 6,328 rooms in well under three years. Considering the difficulties, which ranged from lack of sites to acute shortages of electrical components, and persisted throughout the operation, this must be reckoned no slight achievement. It does not, of course, bear comparison with war-time building feats; but our country is not yet converted to the idea that needs of peace may be as urgent as those of war.

'F.E. AND T.'

The English are often accused, not always unjustly, of doing 'too little too late'. Quite insufficient credit is given to them for the many occasions on which they take action very early and do things on the grand scale. The Further Education and Training Scheme (F.E. and T.) carried through during and after World War II is a good example of the latter.

The purpose of the Emergency Scheme for the Training of Teachers and of the HORSA programme was to set the school system in motion on the lines designed for it by the Education Act of 1944. The purpose of F.E. and T. was to make good the damage done by the war years to the careers of those who had left school.

The planning of this scheme to aid men and women whose higher education or vocational training had been interrupted or deferred by the war began even earlier than that of the Emergency Training Scheme for Teachers. It began in 1941, and the scheme was launched in the early months of 1943. There can hardly have been a more signal illustration of confidence in the country's future offered in those dark days.

Though the President of the Board of Education appointed the inter-departmental committee which did the initial planning, F.E. and T. was not the sole responsibility of his department, nor was its application restricted to England and Wales. It covered the whole of the United Kingdom, and was administered jointly by the Board (later the Ministry) of Education, the Ministry of Labour and National Service, the Ministry of Agriculture and Fisheries, the Scottish Education Department, the Scottish Department of Agriculture, and the Northern Ireland Ministry of Education.

The scheme had a dual purpose: to help individuals, and to help the nation. To help individuals it offered grants for higher education or training to all those men and women who by reason of war service (military or civilian) had had their post-school education or training interrupted or deferred. It aimed to help the nation by ensuring that there should be, despite the war, 'a supply of men and women trained to occupy in the future posts of responsibility in the professions, industry, and commerce'.[1]

As with the Emergency Training Scheme for Teachers the term 'war service' was generously interpreted. So were the terms 'interrupted' and 'deferred'. 'Anyone who was usefully employed, and would otherwise have been studying could at least claim a grant', and 'a candidate for a grant had normally to show only that his studies had been put back by at least a year's interruption caused by his service, or that he was unable to continue his preservice career and needed to be trained for a new occupation'.[2] In numerous cases even greater latitude was shown. In fact, one can almost say that no deserving applicant was refused; certainly, as the Ministry's 1949 report observed,[3] the scheme 'enabled many thousands of young men and women to follow full-time courses at universities and elsewhere who would certainly not have done so in the ordinary way'.

The number of grants made, and especially the high proportion of successful applications, amply confirm the claim that the scheme was generously interpreted. Despite the fact that all applications had to go through two sieves—the Ministry of Labour, which decided whether or not the applicant had made out a *prima facie* claim to a grant, and the Ministry of Education, which decided whether the claim appeared to justify a grant for the course of studies proposed—by the end of 1949 over 83,000 grants had been made. Of the 98,000 applications which by that time had been forwarded to the Ministry of Education only 3,800 had been refused. In all, some 85,000 awards were made, nearly 45,000 of which were for university courses.

---
[1] *Education in 1949.* Report of the Ministry of Education. H.M. Stationery Office, 1950, p. 66.
[2] *ibid.*, p. 67.   [3] p. 67.

All the grants made were for full-time courses, to be taken at a university, university college, or a major college of further education. They were intended to cover all necessary expenses: tuition and examination fees, books and instruments, board and lodging during term time (and vacations if need be), clothes, travelling and incidental expenses. Allowances were made for dependants, and this was extended to cover those of the many students who married while in receipt of grants. Grants to students under the age of 21 at the beginning of a course were adjusted against a parental income scale ranging from £800 to £2,000; but a parent could apply to have the amount of the grant revised at the end of the academic year in which his son or daughter became 21. From students over 21 at the beginning of a course no contribution from parents was required.

To give an idea of actual amounts paid to students the two examples cited in the Ministry's 1949 report[1] may be quoted:

'A single student of over 21 at Oxford or Cambridge, with no other means of his own, who was obliged to maintain himself in lodgings throughout the vacations [or, it may be added, who declared that he did not intend to be supported by parents or relatives during the vacations], would receive in 1949 a maximum grant of £303 a year, together with the payment of tuition and examination fees amounting to, perhaps £80. A married man with a wife and one child, who was obliged to maintain a separate home for them in term time, would receive a maximum grant of, say, £426 a year, together with the payment of his fees.'

There were, of course, some grumbles about the inadequacy of individual grants, and many more about delay in paying them. On the latter score there was during the earlier days of the scheme considerable cause for complaint; as with the Emergency Scheme for Teachers the clerical staff at the Ministry of Education got snowed under. On the former, well, the married student, especially the one with a child or children,

[1] p. 70.

had to be very economical. But the main reason for this was the inflated prices so often charged for lodgings. The single student was, with due care, reasonably well off. Certainly, by comparison with any previous scheme of grants for higher education, F.E. and T. was unequalled for generosity. The cost to the nation was correspondingly high; by the end of 1951, when the scheme had practically run down, about £40,000,000 had been expended on maintenance, and another £12,000,000 on fees.

And the results? In the final analysis these can never be estimated. But at least two things can be said. Had there been no F.E. and T. scheme the teaching, engineering, medical, architectural, and legal professions, among others, would to-day have been in very bad state indeed. Secondly, as the Ministry's 1949 report observed,[1] although F.E. and T. was an emergency measure 'its effects have given a new impetus to the demand for bringing university education within the reach of students who would otherwise be unable to study at a university'. Part, in fact a great part, of the credit for that happy issue must be given to the students themselves, 80 per cent of whom completed their courses satisfactorily. With relatively rare exceptions they applied themselves to their studies with a seriousness and concentration which won deserved praise from their tutors and teachers and did much to bring about an improvement in the attitude of the public towards university studies. Much less has been heard since about 'the idle rich who dawdle through three years at Oxford or Cambridge'. Which is just as well, seeing that the type is now practically extinct.

[1] p. 72.

Chapter Two

PERMANENT STRUCTURE

THE work of building a permanent administrative structure for the new educational system had begun before the Education Act, 1944, was passed, and within a few days after the measure had been placed on the Statute Book the first-fruits of this preliminary labour became apparent. On 10th August Mr. R. A. Butler was appointed England's first Minister of Education. Five days later he issued his first circular,[1] which dealt almost exclusively with immediate administrative matters, the solitary exception being that, as recorded in Chapter One, it announced the postponement of the raising of the school age.

The first necessity was that the machinery prescribed by the Act for central and local administration should be set up in time to be ready to function by 1st April 1945. This was a matter of particular concern to the county authorities, for the Minister told them that they must have drawn up by that date their schemes for putting into operation that novel experiment in delegation of local powers introduced by the Act: divisional administration. He said he would send them shortly a memorandum of guidance on the preparation of such schemes (which he did on 15th September),[2] and would let them know which boroughs and urban districts in their areas had put in claims

---

[1] Circular 1, *The Education Act, 1944*. Dated 15th August 1944.
[2] Circular 5, *Local Administration of Education*. Schemes of Divisional Administration. Dated 15th September 1944.

to be 'excepted districts'. Authorities which desired to do without divisional administration should let him know.

As boroughs and urban districts were allowed until 1st October to lodge their claims for excepted district status, and as these claims had then to be discussed by the Ministry and the local authorities concerned, there would clearly be not much time left for drafting schemes and appointing divisional executives. Actually, boroughs and urban districts applied in such numbers as to render impossible any chance of divisional administration being ready to function generally by April 1945.

Mr. Butler advised all authorities that before April he would issue building and other bodies of regulations, and warned them that in that month they were due to begin preparing their development plans for primary and secondary education. To assist them in this task he would send them a memorandum of guidance.[1] But, 'in view of the considerable burden which will be laid upon Authorities by the preparation of Development Plans', he did not for the time being propose to ask them to start work upon the schemes of further education also demanded by the Act.

Imagination boggles at the idea of what would have happened had the local authorities been required to prepare simultaneously both development plans and further education schemes. In specifying that development plans should be completed within twelve months[2] the draftsmen of the 1944 Act greatly underestimated the time it would take most local authorities to compile these massive and complicated plans. In the event, a bare handful only was completed by the date, 1st April 1946, by which all were expected to be finished. Most authorities were months, and some years, behind it.

Mr. Butler further advised the authorities that by 1st April

[1] This was presumably the ill-fated Educational Pamphlet No. 1, *The Nation's Schools*, published May 1945 but later withdrawn in face of public protests.

[2] There was, admittedly, an escape clause.

1945, every one of them must have adopted an 'agreed syllabus of religious instruction'. This was neither so simple nor so speedy a task as might at first sight appear. Every authority which had not already an agreed syllabus in use had to call a conference constituted in accordance with the provisions of the Fifth Schedule of the 1944 Act, that is, representative of the authority, the teachers, and the religious denominations concerned; and this conference had either to prepare a syllabus or agree to adopt one which had been published by another authority. The latter was, within the time allowed, the only practicable course, but many authorities took it as an interim measure only, and later produced their own syllabuses.

The circular further suggested that the authorities would, 'no doubt, find it convenient to consider the general principles upon which the Instruments and Rules of Management for county primary schools and the Instruments and Articles of Government for county secondary schools required by the Act should be framed', and 'after such consultations as may appear to them to be appropriate, prepare model rules and articles for use in the different types of county schools in their areas'. This task tended to get very much pushed into the background, and had not been completed by some authorities by the end of 1951.

There followed during the next few months a stream of regulations, circulars and administrative memoranda from the Ministry. The first regulations to come, in November, were those for school buildings.[1] They at one and the same time shocked and delighted. Everyone who realized how out of date were most of the school buildings in the country, and the thoroughly bad condition of many, hailed the regulations as earnest of the spirit in which the 1944 Act was to be implemented. But, 'not a single primary, secondary, or special school

[1] *Draft Regulations Prescribing Standards for School Premises.* These were accompanied by Circular 10, dated 14th November 1944, and confirmed on 24th March 1945 (S.R. and O., 1945, No. 345).

building in the area is up to the standard required by the Ministry's Regulations', confessed the London County Council's Education Committee; and few if any were the authorities who could say otherwise.

Early in the New Year came regulations governing the Ministry's grants to local education authorities, the conduct of primary and secondary schools, the granting of scholarships and other awards, and the arrangements for school milk and meals. All these were issued before 1st April 1945. During the same period there were circulars about evacuation, national service, clothes rationing, disposal of surplus stores, staffing of schools, employment of school children in agriculture, provision of educational facilities for civilian patients in hospitals and sanatoria, distribution of orange juice jelly, and—most important—two which explained respectively the new Burnham salary scales for teachers and a new Teachers' Superannuation Act.

Circular 39, *Report of the Burnham Committee, 1945* (23rd March 1945), though one of the shortest ever issued by the Ministry —in its original form it comprised eight lines only—was a historic document. It ran:

'I am directed by the Minister of Education to state for the information of the Local Education Authority that he has now approved under Section 89 (1) of the Education Act, 1944, the scales of salaries submitted to him by the Burnham Committees for (*a*) qualified teachers in Primary and Secondary Schools; (*b*) teachers in Technical Institutions; and (*c*) unqualified and temporary teachers. Copies of the scales so approved will be circulated to Authorities as soon as possible. In the meantime, I am to inform the Authority that the Minister proposes to make an order under Section 89 providing that the remuneration paid by Local Authorities to their teachers shall be in accordance with these scales as from 1st April 1945.—M. G. Holmes.'[1]

The circular was historic for two reasons. It approved an

[1] Sir Maurice Holmes, then Permanent Secretary of the Ministry of Education.

agreement which introduced, for the first time in the history of English education, the principle of a single basic salary scale for all qualified teachers in maintained schools; hitherto there had always been separate, and differential, scales for teachers serving in elementary, secondary, and technical schools. And, again for the first time, it made payment of the agreed scales mandatory upon the local authorities.

The basic scale agreed involved substantial increases in the salaries of those teachers who had previously been serving under Elementary School Regulations, that is, the teachers in the primary and modern secondary schools. Grammar school teachers, who previously had been more highly paid than teachers in elementary schools, came off much less well. Though allowances additional to the basic scale were granted for possession of a university degree and for each year of training beyond the minimum (and a graduate who had been through a University Training Department was credited with two extra years), their salaries were very little increased; in fact, by no more than was considered adequate to compensate for the increased cost of living.

This produced in the grammar schools a feeling of deep dissatisfaction which was to rankle like a running sore throughout the period under survey. A main cause of discontent was the very small allowance made, despite the protests of the grammar school representatives on the Burnham Committee, for possession of a university degree: a single increment (£15 for men and £12 for women) at the minimum of the scale, and two increments (£30 for men and £24 for women) at the maximum. But there were also other grievances, which will be discussed in Chapter Three.

The minimum basic salary was fixed at £300 for men and £270 for women. This rose by annual increments of £15 for men and £12 for women to maxima of £525 and £420 respectively. Fifteen per cent of qualified assistant teachers were to hold posts of special responsibility, which would carry additional allowances ranging from £50 to £100 a year for men and £40 to £80 for women. Head teachers received allowances according to the size of their schools: two, four, six, eight, or ten increments for schools of under 100, 200, 350, 500, and over 500.

Altogether, between 15th August 1944, and 28th March 1945, the Ministry issued five bodies of regulations, forty-one circulars and forty-two administrative memoranda—no inconsiderable feat of staff work. Especially in view of the fact that during this period the Ministry was reorganizing itself. On 6th April 1945, it announced, in A.M. 43, the main changes it had effected. At headquarters the Department had been organized into five main branches: Schools, Further Education, Teachers, Medical, and Information and External Relations. In addition, there were five other branches: Legal, Finance, Awards, Buildings and Priority, and (Teachers') Pensions. A separate division was to deal with teachers' salaries.

As previously, the Welsh Department (created in 1907) remained responsible, under its own Permanent Secretary, for education in Wales and Monmouthshire. For purposes of administrative contact between the central department and the local education authorities there were organized at headquarters for the time being eight territorial divisions, arranged in two regional groups, this disposition later to be expanded into ten divisions in three groups.

From the foregoing it will be seen that Mr. Butler was hardly exaggerating when he said, at Northampton on 13th October 1944, that the Ministry had been 'overwhelmingly busy'. Equally busy were the local education authorities; and both parties were for years to be engaged up to the very limit of their capacity in grappling with three main groups of tasks. These Mr. Butler defined in his Northampton speech as (i) improvisations, to be carried out during what he termed an 'action' period, which he anticipated would extend over one or two years (actually it lasted much longer); (ii) priority measures, and (iii) long-term development.

PERMANENT STRUCTURE

In view of the fierce and persistent criticism to which the Ministry of Education was subjected, from the moment the German war ended in May 1945, for its alleged slowness in getting 'improvisations' (that is, emergency measures) and priority measures under way it is only fair to recall the immense amount of preparatory work which had to be done in war-time conditions and to emphasize that in addition to the immediate tasks there were also the problems of long-term development to be considered. It is greatly to the credit of the Ministry and the local education authorities that, despite the almost overwhelming pressure put upon them for 'action', they nevertheless contrived to give sustained attention to long-term development. Had they not done so, the striking achievements made, for example, in school building from 1947 onwards would have been impossible.

So, too, would the comprehensive planning of educational facilities in their areas which the local education authorities were statutorily required to carry out. Section 11 of the 1944 Act laid down that:

'As soon as may be after the date of the commencement of this Part of this Act (i.e., after 1st April 1945), every local education authority shall estimate the immediate and prospective needs of their area, having regard to the provisions of this Act and of any regulations made thereunder and to the functions relating to primary and secondary education thereby conferred on them, and shall, within one year after that date or within such extended time as the Minister may in any particular case allow, prepare and submit to the Minister a plan (in this Act referred to as a 'Development Plan') in such form as the Minister may direct showing the action which the authority propose should be taken for securing that there shall be sufficient primary and secondary schools available for their area and the successive measures by which it is proposed to accomplish that purpose.'

Precise directions were given in Section 11 about what a

Development Plan was to contain. Authorities were to take into consideration all the schools in their areas available for providing primary and secondary education (that is, voluntary as well as maintained schools), and to specify which of these schools they proposed to continue, the nature of the education to be provided in each school, the ages of the pupils to be educated therein, the alterations, and the estimated cost thereof, which would be required in the premises of any school, and any additional schools that would be required. The plans were to include information about any arrangements proposed to be made with private schools, any arrangements made or proposed to be made to meet the needs of children below the age of 5 and children requiring special educational treatment, and any arrangements made or proposed to be made for providing boarding education and for the transport of pupils to and from school.

Before submitting their plans to the Minister authorities had to consult with the managers or governors of all schools other than county schools, situated within or outside their areas, which in their opinion would be affected by their plans. (These consultations were a fruitful source of delay; they frequently dragged on for months and sometimes for years.)

By Section 42 of the Act the local education authorities were similarly required to prepare and submit to the Minister Schemes of Further Education. These were to cover every kind of educational facilities for persons beyond compulsory school age, except compulsory part-time education in county colleges for young people up to the age of 18 who were not in full-time education, which was to be the subject of a separate scheme, and university education, which is outside the province of the Ministry of Education. In preparing Schemes of Further Education the authorities were to take into consideration any facilities provided in their areas by universities and university colleges, voluntary organizations and other bodies, with whom they were to arrange consultations, as they were also with adjacent local authorities in order to prevent overlapping or gaps in provision. Again, such consultations often consumed what seemed an inordinate amount of time and energy, though the resultant co-operation as a rule justified it.

It was clear from the beginning that the preparation of these Development Plans and Further Education Schemes would involve a stocktaking the like of which for thoroughness had never before been undertaken, or even contemplated. How well aware some authorities were of this is evident from the fact that they got to work on their Development Plans long before the Act was on the Statute Book. But probably even these prescient authorities did not fully realize at the time upon what a gigantic task they were engaging.

In Circular 28 (8th May 1945) Mr. Butler reminded local authorities of their duty to prepare Development Plans. With it he sent them Form 650G, which indicated the various headings under which the plans should be arranged and the information to be furnished under each head. 'It is not intended', said the circular, 'that copies of the Form itself should be used for the purpose of submitting the Plan.' Indeed, no! Every authority would have needed hundreds of copies. When the time came for submitting the plans, many a one could hardly be contained within a massive printed volume.

That the Minister had in view plans for genuinely long-term development is clear from the wording of this circular.

'The review which Authorities are now required to carry out should be comprehensive . . . to include projects the execution of which will be spread over a considerable period. The Plan will necessarily be more precise as regards the work proposed *for the first few years* [my italics], but it is expected that all Authorities will be able to give at least a provisional indication of their proposals covering the development of the educational system in the later years and *the completion of its reform as now contemplated*. [My italics.]'

The local education authorities took the Minister at his word.

They not only set out to make their plans as comprehensive, precise, and detailed as could possibly be desired, but to base them on carefully thought-out general principles.

'It will be seen,' wrote the Director of Education for the County of Durham in a report prepared for his education committee in July 1945,[1] 'that the preparation of a Development Plan requires the Committee's agreement on the principles upon which the plan is to be based as the future of the education of the county for an indefinite period will be moulded by the form that the plan ultimately takes.'

The Planning Sub-committee of the Westmorland County Education Committee, appointed as early as November 1943, submitted three interim reports, of which the first two dealt mainly with questions of principle, and only the third with concrete proposals for the reorganization of primary and secondary education in the county.[2]

'The purpose of this Introduction to the Plan', it is stated in the published version of Liverpool's *Development Plan for Education*,[3] 'is to survey the general principles and indicate the methods adopted by the Authority in applying the statutory requirements to the particular circumstances of the City of Liverpool.' Almost every plan made specific reference to the principles underlying its compilation.

These principles were by no means always the same. But there were two which, it is safe to say, dominated the thinking of every local authority. They can be stated in words concluding the introduction to the Liverpool Plan:[4]

'The Plan is . . . an attempt in the light of existing experience to survey the steps required to implement the Act of 1944 and to ensure that any school building undertaken in

[1] *Basic Principles underlying the Development Plan*. County of Durham Education Committee, Shire Hall, Durham, p. 2.
[2] *Development Plan for Primary and Secondary Education, 1946*. Westmorland County Council, p. 5.
[3] City of Liverpool Education Committee, January 1948, p. 8.
[4] p. 24.

the next ten or fifteen years is in line with the long-term development of the city. The Authority is convinced that the development of education in Liverpool as set out in the Plan is the most effective contribution it can make to the individual well-being of the children and citizens of the city.'

There can be no doubt that every authority strove to put down on paper its ideal organization of primary and secondary schools, the one it considered would most benefit the children who were its care. Most did so without great concern for the ultimate cost; it has been estimated that, at the prices ruling while the plans were being prepared, altogether a capital expenditure of some £800 to £1,000 millions was envisaged.

Nor can there be much doubt that the principal difficulty encountered by most authorities was that of providing against housing and industrial developments and other causes of shifts in population. So impressed with this problem were the authorities for Smethwick and West Bromwich (who drew up a joint Development Plan) that they wrote:[1]

'The Plan is not a detailed undertaking to carry out certain work irrespective of conditions in the future. It is rather to be regarded as an expression of present intention to be reviewed from time to time as the period for definite action approaches in each case.'

On the other hand the North Riding Education Committee felt that after reviewing all considerations affecting its area, including probable shifts of population, it had been able to prepare 'a development plan which, in general, may stand the test, and may not require much modification when it has to be translated into fact.'[2]

Among the purely educational considerations the question of how best to organize secondary education overshadowed all

[1] *Joint Development Plan.* County Boroughs of Smethwick and West Bromwich. June 1946, p. iv.

[2] North Riding County Council Education Committee. *Report of the Education Committee on the Development Plan for Primary and Secondary Education under the Education Act, 1944.* March 1947, p. 5.

others and produced the most varied crop of conclusions. Despite the acute controversy that was raging at the time over the respective merits of a tripartite organization into grammar, modern, and technical secondary schools and of the 'common', 'comprehensive', or 'multilateral' school it is, I think, a fair judgement that on the whole the plans showed little sign of being influenced by doctrinaire opinion or political bias. London was a notable exception; its decision to establish a system of comprehensive secondary schools throughout its area was a party decision, contested at every step by the minority party. But in general, though Labour leaned towards the common school while Conservative and Liberal favoured segregation, there was agreement that organization must be adapted to fit the particular circumstance of the area, and especially to make the best use of the existing schools.

The result was a range of proposals including the utmost variety. To cite but a few examples: London, Middlesex, Swansea, Coventry, and Westmorland decided for comprehensive or multilateral schools—Westmorland, interestingly enough, for small ones of 500–600 pupils. Darlington, Northampton, Rotherham, and Kent, with other authorities, decided against them. Berkshire, Montgomeryshire, the East and North Ridings of Yorkshire, Barrow-in-Furness, and St. Helens were among the authorities which accepted the principle of bilateralism, that is, of housing two of the three main types of education in a single set of premises. The 'school base', a campus containing all forms of secondary education, organized as separate entities but sharing common facilities, was favoured by Bolton, Brighton, Derby, and the Isle of Wight. But probably a majority of the authorities adopted a mixed organization, accepting segregation where existing schools were well established and respected, yet prepared to try out multi- or bilateral schools in districts where development was needed or likely to be in the future.

The arguments whereby authorities arrived at their decisions occupy many pages in the published versions of Development Plans. They offer a fascinating study to anyone interested in the processes by which a national institution in this country grows and is shaped. *The Times Educational Supplement* claimed[1] that the Development Plans showed the 'inestimable advantage in work of this kind of local over central planning'. That is perhaps over-simplifying the situation, for all the authorities had to work within a framework created by Act of Parliament, and all had to have their plans approved by the central authority, the Ministry of Education, which did not hesitate to suggest substantial modifications to many plans while these were being compiled. It is perhaps more correct to say that the plans offered a signally successful example of the virtue of co-operation between centre and locality, resulting in that 'variety within uniformity' which rightly ranks so high among the ideals of British democracy.

Because they took their task so seriously, many of the authorities soon began to realize that they could not complete it within the twelve months allowed by the Act. A few did: Plymouth, Hull, and Salford, for example, announced in January 1946 that their plans had been approved by their education committees. Stoke-on-Trent, Barrow-in-Furness, and Cornwall did so shortly afterwards. But most authorities had by then found themselves hopelessly behind schedule.

Dorset was in particularly bad case. The Education Committee had drawn up a plan which involved the closure of many small village schools. On submitting this to the County Council early in 1946 the committee had it referred back with the instruction that no school with an average attendance of eighteen and upwards was to be closed. As this involved virtually remaking the whole plan, the committee had no option but to ask the Ministry for more time. They were not alone; other similar requests were already coming in.

Miss Ellen Wilkinson, the then Minister of Education, was

[1] 3rd May 1947.

not at first prepared to tolerate much delay. In Circular 90 (8th March 1946) she again reminded the authorities that it was their duty to submit their plans before 1st April. She was aware, she said, 'of the heavy duties placed upon Local Education Authorities in the preparation of the Development Plan'. Nevertheless, 'in view of the importance of the Plan as the basis of educational reorganization and reform and the desirability of determining, without avoidable delay, the status of voluntary schools . . . and the respective responsibilities of Managers and Governors and the Local Education Authority . . . she would be reluctant to contemplate any considerable deferment of the date of submission of the Plan.'

Miss Wilkinson was, however, prepared to grant to any authority which applied for it an extension of time not exceeding three months. For any longer extension a special case would have to be made out. Within two months 119 of the 146 local education authorities had applied for extra time. By 1st April only sixteen complete plans had been submitted to the Ministry, and within the following six months only fifty more arrived. By the end of 1947 there were still twenty plans to come, though it must be added that eleven of the twenty authorities concerned had sent in one or more instalments for approval.

In retrospect it seems astonishing that anyone could have imagined that these comprehensive blueprints for the future organization of primary and secondary education could, except in the most favourable circumstances, have been drawn up in twelve months. Actually, as has been noted, very few were; and among those authorities which submitted their plans to the Ministry during 1946 some at least had begun work on them—as Kent commented on publishing its plan in the autumn—'long before 1st April 1945'.

In view of the enormous amount of time, energy and money consumed in the preparation of Development Plans, and later of Further Education Schemes, the question has often been asked whether these jobs were worth while. Would it not have been wiser, say the critics, to have concentrated solely upon the immediate tasks, which in all conscience were sufficiently numerous and urgent, and to have left consideration of the future—well, to the future? Especially as everyone realized from the start that neither plans nor schemes would ever be carried out exactly as laid down on paper, and that in particular estimates of cost were almost valueless, so unstable were prices.

The answer must be, I think, that the plans and schemes were abundantly worth while, if only because for the first time in the history of English education those responsible for its provision and administration had to think their problem out through its entire range from general principles to the smallest details of cost and equipment. Moreover, despite the pressing immediate tasks, it was the right moment to do this. Hitherto, public education in England and Wales had been built up, if not quite haphazardly as is so often said, at least bit by bit in response to national needs which could no longer be ignored. The Education Act, 1944, was a deliberate attempt—the first ever made—to reassemble these bits and pieces, with others newly added, so as to make of them a coherent, co-ordinated and all-inclusive structure capable of providing for the total educational needs of the nation, up to the point at which the universities took over. But the 1944 Act, like all Acts of Parliament, was an architect's drawing only; before the builders could begin their work the detailed schedules had to be compiled. And it was, I think, to the good that these schedules should be compiled while the first flush of the excited enthusiasm over the drawing lasted, for in the generous warmth of that enthusiasm an ideal material environment for public education was not only glimpsed but translated into the most exact and detailed terms. However much the country may have to retrench those terms remain in black and white as a challenge. It is one of the most encouraging aspects of the educational scene to-day that Ministry, local education authorities and teachers are still responding strongly to that challenge; every call to economy in school building is regarded as a call to produce better goods at lower cost.

Furthermore, to see the matter in another and a cruder light, had the Development Plans and Further Education Schemes not been prepared when they were, they would never have been prepared at all; and English education would have blundered on as before, never quite certain what to provide, or why.

A THOUSAND NEW SCHOOLS

The first argument used by those people who thought the Development Plans a waste of time and energy was 'But they will never be implemented'. As a matter of fact their implementation (dreadful word!) began while many of the plans were still being prepared. The building of new schools got going on a large scale in 1947, and while it would not be correct to say that every one of the 1,000 schools built between then and the middle of 1952 was built in exact accordance with what was specified in the Development Plan for the area, practically none were departures from the general outline of the plan.

The building of permanent schools got off to a slow start. Almost none was done in 1946. Though during that year some £7,000,000 was expended on educational building, hardly any of this went on new construction; the money was spent on 'a miscellany varying from war damage repair, temporary building for the school meals service, the adaptation of buildings for use as emergency training colleges for teachers and small contracts for the relief of overcrowding, to the first small instalments of hutting for raising the compulsory school age.'[1]

One reason why hardly any new schools were started in 1946 was the rush to get new houses built. No one at first paid

[1] *Education in 1947.* Report of the Ministry of Education. Cmd. 7426. H.M. Stationery Office, p. 50.

any attention to those people who argued that, as most new houses were certain to contain children (especially as priority was being given to young married people), wherever houses were being built in numbers, schools ought to be built simultaneously.[1] However, towards the end of the year the new housing estates themselves began to demonstrate the irrefutable logic of this argument. In November the Ministry of Education initiated an 'operational programme' designed to provide in 1947 new schools for new housing estates, and to supplement in some areas the emergency hutting programme for raising the school age.

Unfortunately, although the Ministry devised a procedure which cut by one half the hitherto leisurely process of drawing up and approving plans and letting contracts, schools continued to take an unconscionably long time to build. (Schools in any case take longer to build than houses.) The amount of work approved by the Ministry in 1947 was more than four times as much as in 1946—the estimated cost was £32,000,000 —but only ten new schools (six secondary and four primary) were opened, as compared with nine (three secondary and six primary) in 1946. Actually, to compare these two years is meaningless; several of the schools completed in 1946 and 1947 were begun before the war, and I think I am right in saying that no school begun in either 1946 or 1947 was finished before the end of the latter year. But the figures were disappointing to those people who had expected schools to spring up like mushrooms almost as soon as the plans had been approved.

What was really disheartening was that, because of the 'fuel crisis' of February 1947 and the persistent shortages of labour and materials throughout the year not much more than half the work approved had got started by the end of 1947. In the circumstances the Ministry wisely decided to concentrate all

[1] This difficult problem is discussed at length in the *Eighth Report from the Select Committee on Estimates*, H.M. Stationery Office, June 1953. See Minutes of Evidence.

PERMANENT STRUCTURE

its building resources upon providing accommodation for the increasing number of children of compulsory school age, building schools for new housing estates, replacing schools destroyed or damaged beyond repair by enemy action, and meeting the most urgent needs of technical education. This meant no new buildings to replace old and unsatisfactory ones, nor for nursery schools and classes, community centres, adult education centres and youth clubs. Even the building of canteens for the school meals service, which up till then had been given top priority, was restricted to the smallest amount possible.

This decision, made in the summer of 1947, was widely and strongly criticized, particularly vigorous opposition being offered to the cessation of nursery school building. If one believes in the value of nursery education (as I most fervently do), it is irksome to have to defend the Ministry's policy. Nevertheless, it cannot be gainsaid that the statutory duty of the Government, and of the local education authorities as its agents, is in the first instance to provide for the children of compulsory school age; and the Ministry at least were by mid-1947 well aware that, owing to the large increase in the birth rate during the war years and after, given all the sources of labour and materials they could reasonably hope to command, it would still be a desperate race against time to provide sufficient accommodation to house the already incoming flood of infants, and—a point rarely mentioned but very important—to cope with the considerable shifts of population, especially to new housing estates. By the end of 1952 the issue of this race was still sufficiently doubtful to be impelling many people to advocate the desperate expedient of excluding children from school until they were six.

In 1947 the Ministry's 'operational programme' was supplemented by a 'short-term building programme 1947-48'. This latter, which included all educational building except the 'operational programme', the school meals building programme, and the HORSA scheme, began to get well under way in 1948. This year, indeed, really marks the start of the gigantic effort which was during the following four years to produce more new schools (and far better schools) than had ever been produced in England within a like period before.

During 1948 work to the value of some £10,000,000 was approved by the Ministry, and by the end of it buildings estimated to cost over £8,000,000 had been started. The tally of schools completed remained small; the harvest of this effort was to come in 1949 and succeeding years. It was, however, considerably larger than that of 1947; ten secondary and fifteen primary schools were fully completed, and another thirty schools, though not completed, were taken into partial use. It was a measure of the pressing need for additional accommodation that this practice of occupying part-finished schools became common throughout the country. I have many times since visited schools where children were doing their lessons to the accompaniment of the noise of cement mixers, painters and decorators, electricians and other workmen.

From 1947 the number of children in the schools rose rapidly. In that year it increased by 322,076, or over 7 per cent. This was largely due to the raising of compulsory school age, which accounted for almost 240,000 of the additional pupils. But there was also an increase of 65,962 (nearly 13 per cent) in the number of children aged 5. This was the beginning of the 'bulge', as it was crudely but significantly called, due to the increased birth rate, which was to swell the school population of England and Wales by close on a million (over 20 per cent) during the following seven years. Throughout these years the 'bulge' dictated the policy of new school building; and it will continue to do so until at least 1960.

By the end of 1948 it had become clear that the procedure for approving building plans was, despite the 1947 acceleration, still far too slow. Further drastic changes were accordingly made, to come into operation on 1st January 1949. These were:[1]

[1] See Circular 191, *Educational Building*, dated 16th December 1948.

(i) For building projects estimated to cost £5,000 or over local education authorities need submit to the Ministry for approval only their final plans.

(ii) For projects costing less than £5,000 no formal approval was required, unless a project involved additional teaching accommodation, changes in the organization of a school, or the establishment of a new school.

(As projects in the school meals' building programme received 100 per cent grant from the Ministry, the limit beyond which approval had to be sought was £1,000 for these.)

(iii) A Development Group was to be formed within the Architects' Branch of the Ministry to study new developments and techniques in building, disseminate information about these, and facilitate their use.

From this last move exciting consequences were to follow. The Development Group decided that, in order to carry out the task laid upon it of designing systems of school building which would be speedy, economical and yet productive of genuinely functional premises of good quality, it had actually to build schools; the task could not be successfully accomplished by office work alone. This was an entirely new departure for the Ministry; previously, the building of schools had been exclusively a matter for the local education authorities.

The experiment was restricted to the building of prototype schools; there was no intention that the Ministry should undertake school building on any large scale, or that it should in any way abrogate the functions of the local education authorities. Some half dozen projects only were embarked upon, in each case with the consent and co-operation of the local authority concerned, the procedure being that the authority 'engaged' the Ministry's architects just as it might any private firm or architect. All the projects were chosen from the already arranged building programme of the authority.

Experiments were made with both single- and multi-storey

buildings. In each case the aim was to work strictly in accordance with three principles:

(i) that the system should be flexible enough in application to allow architects to approach the design of each school as an individual problem with its own educational and site conditions;

(ii) that it should reduce site labour to a minimum by relying on prefabrication in the shape of standard components designed to be made in factories, where labour is usually more readily available and can be more productive, and that the components should be specially designed for rapid site assembly;

(iii) that it should enable permanent buildings of good quality to be built.

'Since permanence and quality depend on specifications and skill in design rather than on technique of production and erection', the Ministry added,[1] 'there is nothing incompatible between this aim (i.e., the third of those above) and the requirement that prefabrication be used.'

The first school to be completed (though not the first to be begun) was the Limbrick Wood County Primary School on the outskirts of Coventry, which was taken into use in September 1952. It was a brilliant vindication of the principles outlined above, the imagination of its designers, the skill of its builders, and the spirit of co-operation that can and should exist between the partners in any such enterprise, be it building or any other joint task.

The Limbrick Wood school consists of two separate and self-contained single-storey buildings, one for infants and one for juniors, standing some fifty yards apart on a flat open site several acres in extent. Both buildings were constructed entirely by the 'Bristol' Mark 1A method of permanent aluminium unit construction invented by the Bristol Aeroplane Company (Weston) Ltd. The school was erected in thirteen months, despite the fact that 30 per cent fewer men were employed on the

[1] Ministry of Education *Building Bulletin No. 8*. H.M. Stationery Office, 1952.

site than on any other similar project, and that, as the school was a prototype, the rate of building was not so rapid as could be expected in established conditions. The index of output showed that the rate of building was nevertheless about twice as quick as for the average school built by traditional methods with traditional materials. The cost was within the Ministry's limit of £140 a school place.

All this might have been highly gratifying to the economist, the administrator and the architect but hardly comforting to the teacher if the school had had no more to recommend it than the fact that it was a quickly and cheaply constructed building. Happily, it had much more; in fact, this and the multi-storey buildings the Ministry was building at the same time may well effect a revolution in school building, for they combine with the most modern educational ideas.

The revolutionary departure from tradition at Limbrick Wood was the elimination of almost all corridor space and the inclusion of the space so gained in classrooms and halls. In the centre of each building is the assembly hall, with a dining hall forming, so to speak, an ante-room to it. The classrooms are sited in groups, or 'cells', outside the exterior corners of the hall; in these, too, the principle of a large room with a smaller ante-room has been used. The larger space is for teaching purposes, the smaller for 'free' activities. The whole is beautifully compact, yet gives an air of amplitude which is not illusory, for each of the classrooms has a superficial area of about 800 feet, as compared with the minimum of 520 sq. ft. prescribed by the Ministry's Regulations. The disadvantage of buildings on this pattern is that in wet weather movement between the classroom units has to be through the hall.

Building Bulletin No. 8, issued in October 1952, described one of the Ministry's more ambitious ventures, the construction of a secondary modern school for 600 boys and girls at Wokingham in Berkshire. Though much of this is single-storey it includes one large four-storey block. The structure consists of a steel framework of standardized stanchions and beams fabricated from light sections welded together, the connexions between them being bolted on the site, and cavity walls made up of single-leaf slabs most of which are 3 ft. 4 in. wide and 2 in. high with an over-all thickness of $3\frac{3}{4}$ in. The slabs are bolted to light steel tees and angles, which in turn are bolted to the main frame.

These details are given to illustrate the wide range of materials used in these experiments by the Ministry. There was nothing new in this; the entire range had previously been tried out by the local education authorities, who during these years almost literally used any materials they could lay their hands on to build schools: bricks, stone, concrete, wood, aluminium, steel, and not infrequently combinations of two or more of these materials. Often the plans for a school had to be redrawn because the main material it was intended to use had dropped out of supply, and even more often the building of a school was seriously held up by delay in securing materials or components. In the circumstances it must be reckoned a remarkable feat that by the middle of 1952 over 1,000 new schools had been completed and fully occupied, while over another thousand were under construction.

This book is not intended to be merely a paean of praise for the Ministry of Education and the local education authorities; but credit should be given where credit is due, and bureaucrats get so many blows that it is a genuine pleasure to hand them an occasional bouquet. In the matter of school building between 1947 and 1952 they certainly deserve one. Within the financial limits and the allocations of labour and materials allowed them by the Government they did a remarkable job. In a time of steeply rising prices they cut costs by 45 per cent. They reduced considerably the time of planning and erection, and they improved greatly the design and construction of schools.

MORE AND MORE TEACHERS

The passing of the Education Act, 1944, implied a large permanent increase in the number of teachers. The Emergency Training Scheme, in addition to making good the gaps torn in the ranks of the profession by the war years (when the number of men entering it fell by one-half), met the immediate need for additional teachers caused by the raising of compulsory school age. Thanks to a change in recruitment policy made while the scheme was in mid-stream whereby acceptance of men was halted and the appeal switched to women the Emergency Scheme also did much towards providing teachers to cope with the flood of five-year-olds which began to seep into the schools in 1947.

But the Emergency Scheme was by its very nature a strictly temporary expedient. It was not intended, and could not have been expected, to continue for long. Its sources of supply were extraordinary, and not inexhaustible; in fact, before it ended there were signs that some at least of them were running dry. But they held out long enough to enable the universities, the Ministry and the local education authorities to expand permanent training facilities sufficiently to meet current demands.

The first step towards this end was made in February 1945, when the Ministry offered to the existing voluntary training colleges (which numbered fifty-one out of a total of seventy-six two-year colleges) capital grants covering up to one-half the cost of any major extensions or improvements to their premises. A year later the Ministry, in place of paying *per capita* grants on students in voluntary colleges, undertook to pay the entire cost of approved tuition and boarding fees, receiving back in respect of the latter contributions made by parents in accordance with approved income scales. This ensured that no applicant would be debarred from training for financial reasons, and also guaranteed the voluntary colleges an assured income sufficient to enable them to maintain adequate standards of efficiency and amenity.

At the same time a change of the first importance was made in the financing of training colleges established and maintained by local education authorities. Hitherto, the cost of these had been borne by the local authorities which provided them. These authorities received grant on their expenditure from the Ministry, and recouped themselves to some extent also by the fees they charged to students. But the old system meant that only those authorities which had established colleges were making any substantial financial contribution to a national service, the training of teachers. The arrangement brought into force in 1946 recognized the injustice of this, and made teacher training a national responsibility the cost of which was shared by all the local authorities in proportion to the extent that they benefited from it.

From 1946 the Ministry paid 100 per cent grant to a local authority on its recognized expenditure in respect of the establishment, equipment and maintenance of a training college and any halls of residence attached thereto. Towards this grant every local authority had to contribute. The formula for this contribution was as follows: there was first allocated to an authority an amount bearing the same ratio to the total of the grant for teacher training as the average number of pupils on the authority's registers bore to the total average number on the registers of all authorities; and there was then deducted from the sum allocated a percentage equal to the combined standard percentage of grant for that authority increased by 5 per cent of the sum allocated.

The change at once stimulated the establishment of new colleges by local education authorities. Nine were opened in the financial year 1946–7, and a further ten in 1947–8. As the building of new colleges was virtually impossible, most of these were housed in premises adapted from other uses. Five of those opened in 1948 took over buildings used till then as emergency training colleges; later a dozen more emergency colleges thus passed into permanent use.

By 1948 grants for capital expenditure amounting to over £135,000 had been made to the voluntary colleges, which were able consequently to make many extensions to their premises. There being no shortage of applicants for training, but rather the reverse, the number of students rose rapidly with the increase of accommodation. In the academic year 1948–9 over 9,000 were admitted to two-year courses, as compared with under 5,000 in 1938–9. Numbers continued to increase until 1951, when the university training departments and the training colleges, now grown to 136 in number, were together capable of accommodating some 14,500 students. In that year, however, although a hundred more women were recruited than in 1950, not all the places in women's colleges could be filled; when the academic year 1951–2 began in September there were still some 250 vacancies, out of 8,000 places. A similar shortage occurred in the autumn of 1952, by which time it had become fairly clear that unless the area of recruitment for women could be enlarged the limit of numbers had been reached.

The students were coming from two main sources: the secondary grammar schools, which contributed about two-thirds of the intake, and older men and women (particularly women) who had been following some other occupation since leaving school. As the training colleges were receiving some 60 per cent of all girls who remained at grammar schools until the age of 17 and did not go on to a university, it was abundantly clear that unless more girls could be induced to stay at school beyond the age of 16 that source of supply was as fully tapped as could be. In fact, in view of increasing competition from other professions open to girls, notably nursing, there was reason to fear that teaching might attract a diminishing percentage.

There were similarly grounds for thinking that progressively fewer recruits would be forthcoming from among older men and women. The opportunity to join the teaching profession at a mature age was, save for the rarest exceptions, a post-war innovation. It was reasonable to assume, therefore, that like all novelties it would for a short while attract more than a normal response and that thereafter would come a slump. Moreover, the greater the success in recruiting candidates for teaching direct from school the fewer older people, presumably, who would feel drawn to the profession.

In the circumstances many people urged the Ministry to recruit from the secondary modern schools. There were any number of pupils, especially girls, they argued, who while they might not be able to secure the minimum academic qualifications required for entry to a teachers' training college (passes in five subjects at the Ordinary level in the General Certificate of Education), would nevertheless make admirable teachers of young children.

Other proposals put forward to strengthen the teaching profession were that an apprenticeship scheme, not dissimilar from the old pupil-teacher system, be organized for pupils who left school before 18, or that such early leavers might be employed as assistants to qualified teachers without ranking as teachers or being in any way committed to entering the profession. Both these schemes were tried out, on a very small scale, by several local authorities with, so far as I could learn, very gratifying results. I shall never forget calling, quite unpremeditatedly, at a small village school to find a delightful girl of 15 aiding the mistress with a very mixed group of infants. She was evidently loving the job, and 'I don't know what I shall do when she leaves' said the mistress to me.

Though this threatened shortage of recruits to teaching emphasized a growing national problem—how to fill the increasing number of posts demanding ability and training, up to the end of 1952 no official move had been made towards broadening the field of recruitment for teachers other than the issue of recurrent appeals to girls to stay longer at school. This was not simply because of complacency or dilatoriness. The teachers' associations were, justifiably, uncompromisingly opposed to any scheme which might threaten to 'dilute' the profession and therefore lower its status, and they had perhaps more reason than usual for maintaining a wary attitude towards any proposals which might tend that way.

The decision taken by the Ministry shortly after the end of the war to get rid of the permanent grade of unqualified teacher had been very largely put into effect. This represented a major triumph for the teachers' associations, which had been urging the reform for many years. But the permission granted to local education authorities to appoint 'temporary' teachers, and the appointment to temporary posts in considerable numbers of persons who lacked professional qualifications seemed to suggest the possibility that another sub-professional group might be substituted for that of the uncertificated teacher. Many people outside the profession thought that the teachers were cutting their own throats by rejecting assistance at a time when they were desperately hard pressed. But it should not be overlooked that status—for which teachers have had to fight so long and so tenaciously—is not only desirable in itself but is also among the most powerful of weapons when negotiating salary scales, and that during these years teachers had been exceptionally dissatisfied with the Burnham Committee awards.

The virtual elimination of the uncertificated teacher must rank among the bolder acts of policy carried through during these years. It involved withdrawing from service, at a period of acute shortage of teachers, several hundreds at a time who, though unqualified, were at least experienced, and several score of highly qualified, experienced and able teachers to train them.

It was shortly before the end of the war that the Ministry decided 'as an act of faith, to eliminate the permanent grade of unqualified teacher, and to allow the recruitment of unqualified persons as temporary teachers only'.[1] In Circular 30 (12th March 1945) the Ministry announced that, subject to the condition specified below, the following would be regarded as qualified teachers:

'Teachers who on or after 1st April 1945 have completed not less than five years of service in the capacity of an uncertificated teacher or a full-time teacher in any other type of school covered by the Regulations (i.e., the Draft Regulations for Primary and Secondary Schools, on which this Circular was a commentary) who would have been eligible for recognition as an uncertificated teacher in a public elementary school, provided that they have completed to the satisfaction of the Ministry the special one-year course of training which will be offered to such teachers as soon as they can be spared from the schools and the courses can be made available.'

More precisely, the offer was made to uncertificated teachers with between five and twenty years' service. Teachers with twenty years' service or more were granted automatically, without any obligation to undergo training, the status of qualified teacher. Teachers with less than five years' service were advised, in Circular 114 of 16th July 1946, to defer application until they had completed that amount of service.

Owing to shortage of accommodation in training colleges and the difficulty of sparing the teachers from the schools it was not considered possible to commence these courses for uncertificated teachers until the autumn of 1947. Then, one emergency training college, Exhall, near Coventry, was devoted exclusively to the training of uncertificated women teachers, and places for men and women were reserved in three other emergency and ten permanent training colleges.

From 1,994 applicants (1,863 women and 131 men), 444

[1] Mr. G. N. (now Sir Gilbert) Flemming, then Deputy Secretary to the Ministry of Education, in an address to the annual conference of the National Union of Teachers, 15th April 1952.

(386 women and 58 men) were selected for these first courses. The places were given, in the main, to the teachers with the longest service. All male applicants with fourteen years' service or more were admitted, all women applicants from England with thirteen years six months', and from Wales with fourteen years nine months'. During their period of training the uncertificated teachers received grants on the same basis as students in emergency training colleges, including allowances for dependants. These last were very necessary, as many of these teachers were either married or supporting aged or invalid relatives.

Between 1947 and 1952, 2,625 uncertificated teachers (2,481 women and 144 men), ranging in age from 24 to 55, received training under this scheme. Only five were refused the status of qualified teacher. At 31st March 1952, only 1,913 uncertificated teachers remained in service in maintained primary and secondary schools, out of a total of 219,896 teachers; and this number was further reduced during the course of the year.

These qualifying courses for uncertificated teachers were among the wisest and most humane enterprises undertaken by the Ministry of Education during these years. I was privileged to visit one of the colleges soon after the beginning and again towards the end of a course, and can testify at first-hand to the remarkable change effected in almost all the teachers. 'They are scarcely recognizable as the same persons', the principal told me on the occasion of my second visit, and I found that to be literally true. Many women in particular came to college inhibited, suspicious, with a desperately limited range of interests, and a most obvious sense of inferiority. During their year of training they shed their inhibitions, lost their suspicion, found a whole world of new interests and, most important of all, discovered in themselves capacities they had never hitherto even suspected. With rare exceptions they had, indeed, become new people.

Admittedly, at the college of which I am speaking the teachers were in the charge of a principal with a genius for evoking self-confidence and latent capacity, who had gathered round her an exceedingly able, enthusiastic, loyal and sympathetic staff. But the same transformation—it would hardly be exaggeration to call it miracle—happened elsewhere as well. How was it done? The Ministry of Education's brief account of the scheme in its annual report for 1951 gives some idea.[1]

'The courses were everywhere designed to meet the special needs of teachers who had had long and sometimes isolated experience, many of whom had understandingly some feeling of frustration at having been deprived of those advantages from which their trained colleagues had benefited.'

Many of the colleges which received uncertificated teachers (altogether, fifty-seven participated in the scheme) wisely began, not with formal instruction but 'by offering opportunities for stimulating and broadening experiences, in the arts, in exploration of new and varied environments, and in critical discussion of ideas, especially in education'. At first this procedure baffled many of the students, who kept wondering, and indeed asking, when the course was going to begin? But its liberating influence quickly began to work, and was very evident when more formal work started. Not a few of the teachers had come to college feeling that there was little, if anything, they could be taught about their job after their long years of experience. They came to learn otherwise; one is quoted as having said: 'I wonder what has been happening in my class all these years', and the other observations cited by the Ministry: 'Now I see why . . .' 'Now I feel that the children's work really means something . . .' and so on, I can vouch for as expressing common opinions among the teachers. They saw their job in an entirely new light.

There is only one further comment I would like to add. No professional occupation, and least of all teaching, should ever be allowed to contain a 'depressed minority'. Some of those

---

[1] *Education in 1951.* Cmd. 8554. H.M. Stationery Office, 1952, pp. 34–5.

uncertificated teachers frightened me when first I met them in college. I had met thousands of uncertificated teachers before, but always in their classrooms, where at least they were the rulers, however indifferent, of their own domains. To meet them in the mass, stripped of all the appurtenances of their small authority, was to realize to what a state of subjection being on the fringes of a profession could reduce normal, healthy, ordinary people.

AREA TRAINING ORGANIZATIONS

The elimination of unqualified teachers from the profession was but one item in a far-reaching reorganization of the training of teachers carried through during these years. It is no exaggeration to say that training was placed on an entirely new basis.

The organizational reforms which were effected derived from the Report of the 'McNair' Committee on the recruitment and training of teachers and youth leaders,[1] which, as recorded on the last page of the fifth edition of *Education in Transition*,[2] was published on 3rd May 1944. It is among the ironies of history that the most important of these reforms resulted from the one recommendation which was not unanimous.

Exactly half the Committee recommended that the universities should accept full responsibility for all teacher training throughout England and Wales. They wanted the universities to set up 'Schools of Education' which should be, in their own words,[3] 'organic federations of approved training institutions working in co-operation under the aegis of the university'. The other half of the Committee wished to retain, in somewhat improved form, the existing system whereby the University

[1] *Teachers and Youth Leaders.* H.M. Stationery Office, 1944.
[2] In which a chapter bringing the story down to the passing of the Education Act, 1944, was substituted for the Epilogue in the previous editions.
[3] p. 54.

Training Departments and the Training Colleges functioned separately, a limited amount of liaison being maintained between them by the Joint Examining Boards set up in 1930.

The respective merits of these two proposals, which became known as 'Scheme A' (Schools of Education) and 'Scheme B' (Joint Examining Boards), were vigorously debated during the following two years. It is probably a fair generalization to say that on the whole the local education authorities and the teachers favoured Scheme A while at first the universities desired Scheme B or some modification thereof. What at any rate emerged from the numerous discussions, formal and informal, was that not all universities welcomed the idea of shouldering the responsibility implied by Scheme A. Instead, they proposed a 'Scheme C', under which the 'School of Education' (or 'Institute of Education', as it came to be more generally called), while centred on the university town, would be a separate and autonomous entity and not a part of the university. It would be established by a Declaration of Trust and wholly financed by the Ministry of Education; and the university's interest in it would be confined to representation on its governing body along with the local education authorities and the colleges and training departments concerned.

In Circular 112 (11th June 1946) the Minister of Education agreed to the setting up of different kinds of 'Area Training Organizations' (A.T.O.) in the various university regions—or in other words agreed to let universities choose Scheme A, B, or C as they felt inclined. Thereafter constitution making went ahead steadily. Interestingly enough, when it came to the point, nearly all the universities decided for Scheme A. Four A.T.O.s were set up in 1947, by the Universities of Birmingham and Bristol and the University Colleges of Nottingham and Southampton.[1] All were of the Scheme A pattern. Ten more followed in 1948, based on the Universities of Durham, Leeds,

---

[1] Now both full universities.

London, Manchester, Reading, Sheffield, and Wales, and the University Colleges of Exeter, Hull, and Leicester.[1] Of these all except Reading were Scheme A. Cambridge and Liverpool Universities, like Reading, opted for Scheme C; Institutes of Education were established in these cities in 1949.

Thus by mid-1949, only five years after the publication of the McNair Report, the organization of teacher training throughout England and Wales had been completely transformed. Instead of there being two separate systems, one controlled and directed by the universities and university colleges and the other by the Ministry of Education, there was now a single system for which the responsibility was shared by sixteen Area Training Organizations, for thirteen of which the universities and university colleges had accepted full financial and administrative responsibility. Only one university remained outside the new system; and happily Oxford finally decided to come in. A University Institute of Education was established there in 1951.

The areas covered by the A.T.O.s vary widely in size. The number of member institutions affiliated to a School or Institute of Education also differs greatly; London has thirty-seven, Exeter and Hull have three each, and Oxford only two. Most of the A.T.O.s, however, have from half a dozen to a dozen institutions and cover an area with a radius of roughly fifty miles. The constitutions of the A.T.O.s all vary in detail, but not substantially except that the financial basis of the three non-university institutes is fundamentally different from that of the university institutes and schools. These three are, as was proposed in Scheme C, financed by a 100 per cent grant from the Ministry of Education. At some universities the Professor of Education is also the Director of the Institute or School, but more frequently the latter is a separate post, which in some cases carries professorial rank.

[1] Leicester's responsibility is partial only. For purposes of training and examination its member institutions are affiliated also to Birmingham.

PERMANENT STRUCTURE

An Area Training Organization is entrusted with five main functions. These may be defined as follows:

(i) To supervise the courses of training in member colleges and to further their work in every possible way.

(ii) To recommend to the Ministry of Education for the status of qualified teacher students who have successfully followed courses of training in member institutions, both training colleges and university departments of education.

(iii) To plan the development of training facilities in the area.

(iv) To provide an education centre for students in training, teachers serving in the area, and other people interested in education.

(v) To provide facilities for further study and research, and refresher courses for qualified teachers.

By 1952 all the A.T.O.s were fully engaged in carrying out these functions. Each had its Professional Board, representative of all the member establishments and the university, for the oversight of curricula and the conduct of examinations. Working under the direction of the Professional Boards were Boards of Studies, each responsible for preparing and revising syllabuses in one subject. Most Professional Boards had also attached to them a board for further studies, a research committee, and an editorial board in charge of publications. Nearly all the A.T.O.s were already publishing quarterly research publications, several were also publishing occasional more substantial volumes, and some had in addition a 'house journal' for the dissemination of news and views.

Every A.T.O. had secured a home for its institute, usually in premises previously used for other purposes, though Southampton University had a very fine new building. As a rule the accommodation in an institute included lecture rooms, smaller rooms for group discussions or committee meetings, offices for the staff, a canteen and a library. Some of the libraries contained by 1952 fairly large and well-chosen selections of standard and reference works and professional publications; many had also good representative collections of current textbooks.

The staffs of the institutes varied greatly in size. London's was by far the largest, with six professors and two readers, and appropriate secretarial and clerical staff. The smaller institutes had almost all at least a director, a tutor, a research officer, a librarian, a secretary, and a clerk. Two institutes, Birmingham and Bristol, had two professors of education; two had as many as six staff tutors. Others had added to the minimum establishment research Fellows, research assistants, assistant librarians, and so on.

The provision of such an education centre as an institute, at the service of students, teachers and interested members of the lay public, had never before been the specific responsibility of any body. Nor had the systematic provision of refresher courses for serving teachers and of facilities for them to engage in further study and research while actively engaged in teaching. Many of the A.T.O.s had done much in both these directions by 1952. During the academic year 1950–1, for example, Birmingham organized conferences, lecture courses and exhibitions of books and teaching aids, Leeds arranged conferences and courses and did a survey of modern schools in its area, Manchester organized no fewer than thirty-eight courses for teachers.

Several institutes had established longer courses for teachers leading to Diplomas in Education. Leeds had instituted four such diplomas: in Primary Education, Secondary Education, Religious Education, and Educational Administration. Almost all the institutes had engaged upon a considerable body of research, upon such varied topics as 'The Balance between Activity and Attainment in the Primary School', 'The Remedial Treatment of Reading Disability', 'The Social and Mental Development of the Adolescent', and 'The Use of English in Latin Teaching in England in the Sixteenth Century'.

PERMANENT STRUCTURE

The institutes are yet young. No one can yet foretell what mark they will make upon the development of English education, though one may safely hazard the guess that it will be an important one. A friendly Australian observer[1] who was by no means afraid to offer criticisms was able to write at the end of a tour of them in 1951 that 'My impression gained through visiting all the Institutes was that they all exemplified vitality, they all had the "vision of greatness", and they were all seized with the necessity of studying the deeper issues involved in their work'. Of not all newly founded institutions is it possible to say anything like so much of good.

[1] Professor R. G. Cameron, Professor of Education in the University of Western Australia.

Chapter Three

EXPERIMENT IN SECONDARY EDUCATION

By far the most important single reform introduced by the Education Act, 1944, was the extension of secondary education to all children. This was fundamental, in two respects; it indicated a determination to raise the educational and cultural standards of the nation as a whole, and it marked a final departure from the tradition, hitherto persistent throughout the whole of English history (though weakening rapidly during the past half century), that education beyond the elementary stage is a privilege to be reserved to the dominant élite—be it of wealth, power, intellect, or whatever else fashion may dictate.

It is much too early yet for anything approaching the full effects of this reform to have made themselves felt. That will take several generations. It will be many years before we have even learned how to give all children a secondary education that is genuinely suited to their 'ages, abilities, and aptitudes'. All that can be said at present is that, considering the exceptional difficulties which beset all education during the years immediately following the war, we seem to have made a modestly successful start.

Much encouraging experimental work has been done in the new secondary schools, and in not a few of the older-established grammar schools. By 1952 tentative lines of advance were here and there beginning to define themselves. Whether or not these will prove to be sound the future has yet to determine./

Perhaps the fact that no drastic changes were attempted at the moment of change-over from the old system to the new was the best augury for ultimate success. April 1st 1945, was unmarked by any substantial alterations in the life and work of the schools. There were no public celebrations even, though doubtless many Heads of newly promoted secondary schools addressed their pupils on the opening day of the summer term, telling them of their more exalted status, and in true English fashion urging them to live up to it. Otherwise, when the 3,000 or more maintained and assisted schools for 'senior pupils'[1] became officially secondary modern schools an outside observer would have been at a loss to detect any difference. There were the same pupils and the same teachers in the same buildings using the same books and equipment and, since the raising of compulsory school age was still two years ahead, in most cases following the same curriculum.

Any idea that, when 'D-day for the schools' arrived, thousands of teachers straightway took from their desks new curricula and immediately launched them on their pupils can be dismissed at once. Educational reform does not happen that way in England. Even when introduced by Act of Parliament, reform, as distinct from administrative reorganization, remains a process of gradual and often apparently haphazard advance, faster here, slower there, never entirely ceasing, yet never making any spectacular leaps ahead. Legislative or administrative change, even when of such moment as the promotion of the senior elementary schools to secondary status in 1945 or the raising of compulsory school age from 14 to 15 in 1947, does little more at the moment than give added encouragement and impetus to curricular change. In other words, it lays the foundation for the new edifice but does not erect the super-

[1] 'All-age' schools, containing both junior and senior pupils, were for the sake of administrative convenience still ranked as primary schools.

structure. That is done brick by brick, by the people in the schools. English education is intensely personal and individualistic; its character and quality depend at any given time more upon persons and less upon the system than does the education of any other country I know.

What did happen on 1st April 1945, was that an unknown number of elementary school teachers took a deep breath, squared their shoulders and said to themselves: 'I'm Elementary no longer; I'm Secondary. And whatever the odds I'll see to it that my youngsters get at least something like a secondary education.' That is no doubt putting the matter melodramatically; probably few teachers actually uttered such words (though some certainly did, for I heard them), but they expressed the unspoken thoughts of thousands.

There were, admittedly, many teachers who said—or thought —'It'll make no difference; it's a change in name only.' There were others who were at the time too tired or too indifferent to bother much whether it mattered or not; and these were not all either lazy or incompetent teachers. They included some who were temporarily drained of vitality by the magnificent efforts they had made during the war, and some who, having had their hopes frustrated so many times before, could not at once realize that the longed-for day of promise had at last arrived. But for a great host of ex-elementary school teachers 1st April 1945, meant a tremendous spiritual uplift. Only those who have known the English elementary school system from the inside can fully understand what that day meant to those men and women.

Though little or no outward sign marked the onset of secondary education for all, much was in fact happening below the surface. Many a teacher was giving anxious thought to the problem of how to transmute an elementary into a secondary education, and most local education authorities were actively grappling with two of the most difficult conundrums presented by secondary education for all when this has also to be suited to 'ages, abilities, and aptitudes': how to ensure that on entry pupils will be placed in suitable courses, and what kinds of schools are best fitted to provide the wide variety of courses that is needed.

About the second of these problems there was very little in the way of action that the authorities could take at the moment. However much they might desire to remodel their existing network of post-primary schools they had not the means to do so; willy-nilly, they had to carry on with the buildings at their command and the teaching staffs in their service. This was a problem to be worked out in their Development Plan, a question of what they hoped to do in the more or less distant future. But the first problem was immediate; and it was quickly complicated by a circumstance which should have been foreseen but in too many places was not—or perhaps it would be more accurate to say that it had been buried beneath a wave of wishful thinking.

SELECTION FOR SECONDARY EDUCATION

Before 1944 the 'Special Place' examination at 11 plus had been designedly an instrument used for selecting children suitable for grammar school education, to which these children proceeded with all the aura of scholarship winners. Many people imagined that the introduction of secondary education for all would put an end to the previous intense competition for entry to grammar schools. Nothing of the sort; in many places the competition if anything increased.

Numerous parents—and it must be emphasized that on the whole these were among the most intelligent parents, deeply concerned for their children's future—simply refused to regard the new secondary schools as secondary schools or to believe that they would ever be capable of giving secondary education. They did not understand their purpose, and they made no attempt to do so. The grammar schools, on the other hand, they both knew and trusted; they knew the social and intellectual prestige they carried and the opportunities they offered, through 'Matric', of securing respected, relatively well paid, and above all secure employment. And they realized, with something akin to panic, that they could no longer get their children into grammar schools by payment of fees if they 'failed the scholarship', and they believed that this meant an end to all hopes of professional careers, that is, to the type of career most respected by the middle classes.

The Vice-Chancellor of Reading University accurately portrayed the feelings of many such parents in a book[1] which he published in 1952.

'Paul says that he is determined that the child shall not go to the Secondary Modern School, that the damn place is only an elementary school really and that he's not going to have his daughter labelled at the idiotically early age of eleven as the kind of half-wit who is not capable of being what he calls "normally and decently educated". He seems to think that the child has been as good as certified M.D. . . . '

Most parents who felt thus could not afford, however, to do as Mr. Wolfenden's Paul did: send his daughter to an expensive private boarding school. Yet they were determined, and many still are, by hook or by crook to get their children into grammar school. They naturally resorted to the expedient so widely used in pre-1944 days: intensive coaching of their children for the '11 plus exam'. A report published by the Bristol University Institute of Education[2] in 1952 disclosed that of the new entrants to two Wiltshire grammar schools 65 per cent had been coached, either privately or in their primary school, for the entrance examination. Such a proportion may well be typical. (It does not imply that 65 per cent

---

[1] *How to Choose your School*, by J. F. Wolfenden. Oxford University Press, pp. 5–6.
[2] *Studies in Selection Techniques for Admission to Grammar Schools.* University of London Press, p. 21.

of all primary school children were, or are, coached for this examination, but only 65 per cent—or whatever the proportion may happen to be—of those who are regarded, either by their parents or their teachers, as having a chance to secure a place in a grammar school.) The effects of this widespread systematic coaching were undoubtedly substantial, as Professor P. E. Vernon of London University and other investigators have shown. 'The average rise (in a child's Intelligence Quotient) after coaching,' Professor Vernon has stated,[1] 'is about 14 I.Q. points, ranging up to 18 points in brighter and entirely unsophisticated pupils, but down to 9 points in duller and more experienced classes.' Such rises must have materially affected many lists of those selected, or rejected, for grammar school.

Though it was only a minority of parents which felt and acted thus, their attitude was certainly among the factors which induced local education authorities to apply themselves conscientiously, thoroughly, and often with much ingenuity to the task of securing that their procedures for allocating children to the different kinds of secondary education should be not only accurate but as obviously fair as possible. I do not think it was the main factor. This I believe to have been a sincere desire to give, so far as lay within their power, the most suitable form of secondary education to every child. I have no patience with those people who indulge in wholesale accusations against the authorities of indifference to the interests of the children or contempt for the feelings of parents. In most cases the exact opposite is the truth; quite naturally, seeing that 'authorities' are made up of men and women who are themselves fathers and mothers, no less imbued with parental feelings than any other parents.

From the start the local authorities took the task of allocating children to secondary schools with the utmost seriousness. It

[1] Article in *The Times Educational Supplement*, 1st February 1952, later included in a pamphlet, *Intelligence Testing*, published by *The Times*.

is safe to say that more experiment, investigation and research was done between 1944 and 1952 upon selection for secondary education than upon any other educational problem, and that most of it was either done by or at the instigation of the local education authorities.

The authorities' main problem, in fact, one might say their only serious problem, has always been, and still is, to discover how to come to a right decision about the 'borderline cases', that is, the often numerous children about whom, when all the normal tests and inquiries have been made, there is still an element of doubt. At least half, and usually more, of the children tested in any given year cause the authorities no trouble at all, provided the accommodation in their secondary schools matches up to the results given by the tests. (Unhappily, it too often does not.) The top 25 per cent or so and the bottom 25 per cent select themselves automatically. The 50 per cent in the middle often present a formidable problem.

Two early attempts[1] to solve this problem may be cited as illustrating the care authorities take over it. In Devon the authority, by way of experiment, held in 1945 two written examinations, each consisting of standardized tests of intelligence and of attainment in formal English and arithmetic. The first of these examinations was taken by all the children due to move up into secondary school, the second by all except those who had done exceptionally well or badly in the first. After the examination papers had been marked a circular letter was sent to the head teachers of the primary schools asking them to draw attention to children who in their opinion had not done themselves justice. These children were given a further test, of a novel and original character. They were assembled, in small groups of about eleven to sixteen, and kept under skilled observation for the whole of a day, during most of which they were occupied in games and other activities designed to reveal

[1] Both reported in *The Times Educational Supplement*, on 27th July and 5th October 1946, respectively.

their natural abilities, aptitudes and interests. This procedure was still in operation in 1952, when the authority published a further account of it.[1] Its aim had been expanded from assessment of a few children to cover the entire borderline group, and the results were said to be equally satisfactory.

Very different after the first stage was the procedure tried out in 1946 by Southend-on-Sea. Like Devon, this authority began by putting all the children in the age group through three standardized tests, of intelligence, English and arithmetic. The results of these tests were considered along with reports by the primary school head teachers. Then the parents' desires for their children were ascertained.[2] Finally, all children about whom doubt was still felt (the genuinely 'borderline' cases) were interviewed by a panel of teachers and administrative officers. In extreme cases a psychologist was called in to give individual tests.

There were many other interesting variations. In its Report for 1951 the Ministry of Education, which had asked the authorities for statements of the basis on which they allocated pupils to the different forms of secondary education, summarized the position fairly by saying[3] that 'The main impression given by these statements is a remarkable uniformity in matters of administration combined with much variety in the techniques of assessment.' 'The main emphasis', said the Ministry, 'is placed by authorities on intelligence tests, usually combined with tests in arithmetic and English.' But 'school reports, especially in borderline cases, give scope for taking into account the child's record and character.'

The normal age for transfer from primary to secondary education, the Ministry found, was between 11 and 12, though

[1] *Education*, 31st October 1952.
[2] In view of the widespread belief that *all* parents want their children to go to grammar school, it is interesting to note that in 1946 nearly 60 per cent of Southend parents did not. Over one-third preferred the modern school, and almost one-quarter the technical secondary school.
[3] *Education in 1951*. H.M. Stationery Office, 1952, p. 11.

some authorities allowed exceptionally able children to transfer between 10 and 11,[1] and most allowed 12-year-olds to sit the tests if they had been unable by reason of illness or other unavoidable cause to take these previously. In almost all areas all children in the appropriate age group who were attending maintained schools were tested, and children at independent schools were offered the chance of sitting the tests. In the case of children who, after taking the examination, moved from the area of one local authority to another the award of the examining authority was usually accepted without question. But nearly all the authorities refused to accept the results of tests taken abroad.

Most authorities gave one series of tests only, except to 'borderline' children. Nearly all gave arithmetic, English, and intelligence tests. Some added a test of composition (this form of testing has had an interesting history of general use, general abandonment, and tentative reintroduction). No authority interviewed all the children, and about one-third interviewed none. In cases of doubt, or of discrepancy between the results of various tests, authorities were tending to turn more and more to the primary school head teachers for advice. Some authorities were conducting systematic follow-up inquiries to assess the success of their transfer procedures, and all had arrangements for the transfer at a later age of children who appeared ill-suited in the type of school to which they had been sent.

WHAT KINDS OF SCHOOL?

During the period under review the great bulk of secondary education in England and Wales was conducted in three separate and distinct types of schools: grammar, modern, and technical. By 1952, however, there were signs which suggested that this tripartite organization might shortly begin to give way

[1] As had been sanctioned by the Education (Miscellaneous Provisions) Act, 1948.

to one comprising a larger variety. The grammar school was holding its own, and was indeed in a stronger position than in 1944, but the technical secondary school seemed to be slowly losing ground, while the modern school was developing a number of interesting variants, including amalgamations with other types.

Tripartitism was a natural result of the historical evolution of post-primary education in England and Wales. The grammar school—oldest by many centuries of English schools—had never been other than a secondary school. The public elementary school, almost from the day of its birth, strove to give its older and abler pupils something more than an elementary education. In 1926 the Consultative Committee of the Board of Education, in its Report on *The Education of Adolescent* (the 'Hadow' Report), recognized that these efforts had produced a genuine form of secondary education and recommended that the senior part of the elementary school (i.e., all pupils aged 11 and upwards) be given secondary status under the name of the modern school.

In the early years of the twentieth century technical colleges began to provide day classes for ex-elementary school pupils which would prepare them for immediate entry into various forms of industrial and commercial employment, and in 1913 these were recognized for grants by the Board of Education as Junior Technical schools. In 1938 the Consultative Committee, reporting on *Secondary Education with special reference to Grammar schools and Technical High schools (the 'Spens' Report)* recommended that these too (or at least some of them) be granted secondary rank. A Committee of the Secondary School Examinations Council appointed by the then President of the Board of Education, Mr. R. A. Butler, in 1941 (the 'Norwood' Committee) to re-examine the curriculum and examinations in secondary schools in the light of the proposed recasting of the statutory system of public education, in 1943 confirmed the judgement of the 'Spens' Committee, as against that of the 'Hadow', by recommending a tripartite and not a bipartite (grammar and modern) basis for secondary education.

The Coalition Government accepted the recommendation of the 'Norwood' Committee that secondary education should be organized on a tripartite basis, and declared in their White Paper, *Educational Reconstruction*, published in July 1943, that 'Such, then, will be the three main types of secondary education, to be known as Grammar, Modern, and Technical.'

This decision did not get by without protest. For many years there had been a considerable body of professional and public opinion in favour of what was variously termed the 'Multilateral', 'Comprehensive', or 'Common' secondary school,[1] that is, a single school which would receive all children of secondary age from a given geographical area and provide for them a suitable variety of courses. That was in 1943, and was still in 1952, the official policy of the Labour Party.

It is important to note that no mention of a tripartite, or any other precise form of organization of secondary education, occurs in the Education Act, 1944. This requires (Section 8 (1)) only that there shall be 'sufficient schools' for providing primary and secondary education, and defines 'sufficient' as:

'... sufficient in number, character and equipment to afford for all pupils opportunities for education offering such variety of instruction and training as may be desirable in view of their different ages, abilities, and aptitudes, and of the different periods for which they may be expected to remain at school, including practical instruction and training appropriate to their respective needs.'

Nevertheless, the Ministry of Education repeated its assertion that secondary education would be organized in the three

[1] These three terms, of which 'Multilateral' was the most commonly employed, were generally used as though synonymous until mid-1947, when the Ministry, in Circular 144 (*Organization of Secondary Education*, 16th June 1947), gave them precise definitions. A multilateral school is one organized in three clearly defined sides, a comprehensive school one not so organized. The term 'Common' could cover either, but has been largely discarded.

types of schools in *The Nation's Schools* (May 1945), the first of a continuing series of educational pamphlets, and again in the second, *A Guide to the Educational System of England and Wales.* It must be added that neither in *Educational Reconstruction* nor in any subsequent publication did the Ministry suggest that this was to be a rigid or indeed the only form of organization. Its attitude from the start was that:

'It would be wrong to suppose that they [i.e., grammar, modern, and technical schools] will necessarily remain separate and apart. Different types may be combined in one building or on one site as considerations of convenience and efficiency may suggest.'[1]

Later the Ministry became even more cordial than this towards deviations from tripartitism, and enlarged its idea of their possible varieties; but it never departed from its adherence to the tripartite basis.

On 19th July 1944, the Education Committee of the London County Council, at a memorably—and exceedingly lengthy!—meeting held in the basement of County Hall, resolved to recommend to the Council that 'the post-primary part of the Council's Development Plan . . . should aim at establishing a system of Comprehensive High Schools throughout the County of London . . .'[2]

Ironically enough, that decision probably did more than any other single cause to sway the balance of professional and public opinion against comprehensive and multilateral schools. For the London proposal envisaged the establishment of about a hundred schools containing up to 2,000 pupils or even more. Almost everyone jumped to the conclusion that a comprehensive or multilateral school must necessarily be of such size, despite the fact that the 'Spens' Committee (which rejected the idea of multilateralism) had put it[3] much more modestly at

[1] *Educational Reconstruction*, p. 10.
[2] Agenda Paper dated 19th July 1944, p. 17.
[3] Report, p. xx.

'say 800 or possibly larger'. All the Englishman's innate distaste for large schools welled up, and the idea of the comprehensive school has never quite recovered from the blow dealt it when England's largest municipality decided to adopt it.

Even some people not entirely averse from the idea of trying out the comprehensive, or the multilateral, school, criticized the London County Council for embarking upon a total policy of comprehensive schools instead of beginning by setting up one or two as experiments. Actually, as those who drew up the London plan were well aware, there was no possible chance of launching the policy on a large scale. In the event, its development was even slower than they anticipated. As has been recorded in Chapter Two, new school building between 1945 and 1952 was entirely restricted to housing the additional school population, supplying new housing estates with schools, and replacing schools destroyed by enemy action. However much the London County Council had desired to set up all their comprehensive schools at once, or quickly, this would have been physically impossible. In 1947 the Council established some half dozen quasi-comprehensive schools by grouping neighbouring schools under a single head, but by July 1952 no building for a comprehensive school had been completed, and only three were under construction.

Much the same state of affairs obtained in other areas where comprehensive schools had been mooted. About one-third of the local education authorities included in their Development Plans proposals for comprehensive or multilateral schools: a few, such as Coventry and Swansea, throughout their areas, but most in selected districts only. Few of these proposals had matured by 1952. The necessity to provide places for the increasing school population meant that new building had to be concentrated largely upon primary schools, of which approximately three were built for every one secondary school. By the end of 1952 there were still fewer than a score of comprehensive schools in the country and only one or two multilaterals. There were, however, fifty or more bilateral schools, that is, schools providing two of the three types of education, and others were being planned, especially in rural areas. Of these bilaterals more than two-thirds were grammar-modern schools.

In one area, Middlesex, organized opposition by parents and teachers reduced by one-half the authority's proposed experiment with comprehensive schools. The county wanted to start six. Protest meetings were held, resolutions and petitions sent to the Ministry, and questions asked in Parliament. No doubt this was not the only reason which determined the Minister to reduce the scale of the experiment; but whether or not that be so only three schools were sanctioned.

It may well be that the restrictions upon school building between 1945 and 1952 affected permanently the structure of English secondary education. There can be little doubt that had the local education authorities been able to build secondary schools as and where they wished in, roughly, 1946 to 1948, there would have been many more experiments with comprehensive and multilateral schools. As it was, the modern secondary school was given seven valuable years in which to prove its worth; and on the whole it made excellent use of the time.

'SECONDARY MODERN'

At 1st April 1945, the date on which they became officially secondary, there were approximately 3,000 senior elementary schools housed in their own buildings or, if they shared premises, organized as self-contained departments under their own Heads. They contained about 750,000 pupils between the ages of 10 and 14, and a few thousands over 14; and they were staffed by approximately 34,000 teachers. There were also about 8,800 'all-age' schools, that is, schools containing children of all ages from 5 or under to 14 and over. Of these the 'Senior' classes (i.e., those containing children aged 12 and upwards) also became officially secondary, though the schools were, for the sake of administrative convenience, still ranked as primary. In these senior classes there were about 400,000 children.

At the same date there were about 1,200 maintained or assisted secondary grammar schools and 166 Direct Grant grammar schools, containing together about 575,000 pupils, of whom about 265,000 or almost half, were aged 14 and upwards. Just over 300 junior technical and junior commercial schools and junior art departments became secondary technical schools. These contained some 65,000 pupils, of whom about 43,000, or more than two-thirds, were 14 years old and upwards. The high proportion of older pupils was due to the fact that these schools had a later entry age—usually 12 or 13—than grammar or modern schools. Few of their pupils were over 15.

It will thus be seen that at the time of the change-over the children in the modern and all-age schools made up almost two-thirds of the total of all children of secondary age. Of secondary school children of compulsory school age they constituted almost three-quarters. When the school leaving age was raised both these proportions became slightly higher.

I have set out these figures in order to underline the very large size of the modern school, and the consequent magnitude of the experiment the country was undertaking in bringing at one stroke such a huge number of children within the province of secondary education. Critics of the modern school— and they are many—are prone to overlook the fact that until 1945 the one million or more children in modern and all-age schools had been receiving an elementary education, in buildings designed and equipped for elementary work, from teachers most of whom had been trained for that work and for no other. Not until 1946-7, when teachers began to arrive in numbers from the emergency colleges, did the modern school have any staff specifically trained for the type of secondary work it was created to do.

The critics are apt also to overlook a second important fact: that the modern school did not really begin its career as a secondary school until September 1948. Only then, when for the first time it contained a full complement of 14-year-old children, was it able to plan and carry through a four-year course. By the end of 1952 the modern school was in a very real sense only just over four years old.

It is true that in another sense the birth of the modern school may be put back to thirty years before 1948, to the Education Act, 1918, which, by instructing local education authorities to provide courses of advanced and practical instruction in senior elementary schools, set those schools firmly on the road to secondary status. But it is, I think, more accurate to regard those thirty years as a prolonged period of gestation. The senior elementary schools, however striking the advance of some of them may have been, were still *elementary* schools, hampered by regulations which effectively prevented them from being genuinely secondary.

If then the birth of the modern school be accepted as September 1948, one has to record that this was not accomplished without moments of anxiety and even of danger. Though the Ministry of Education never faltered (at least outwardly) in its conviction that all would be well, the race to assemble sufficient accommodation and staff to cope with the 'extra year' was only won by a desperately short head. During 1946, when both HORSA huts and emergency trained teachers appeared to be forthcoming in quite inadequate numbers, more and more people, including some who ardently desired the reform, began to doubt whether it would be wise to attempt to raise the school leaving age so early as 1947.

The late Miss Ellen Wilkinson, then Minister of Education, did nothing to allay these doubts when, in commendably courageous but distinctly tactless words, she declared at Oxford in January 1946 that to do so was 'an act of faith rather than an act of wisdom'. A month later, at a meeting in Surrey, she committed herself unguardedly to the statement that 'the school leaving age will be raised on 1st April next year whether or not the teachers are there or the classrooms are there'. This statement, which was given wide publicity in the Press, led not unnaturally to some awkward questions in the House of Commons.

That was but a piece of political gaucherie which did not materially affect the issue. But there was later a brief period during which the raising of the school age seemed seriously threatened. Powerful voices were raised to prevent it. The country's economic plight, they said, was desperate. Every possible pair of hands was wanted in industry, and it would be 'flagrantly foolish', in the words of one of them,[1] to keep out of employment over 300,000 young persons for a year at this time of Britain's direst need.

But the Labour Government were not to be shaken out of their resolution. This was a reform for which their Party had striven for fifty years, and now that at long last they had it within their power to bring it about nothing short of complete national collapse was going to prevent them. In fact, raising the leaving age to 15 was for them but the half-way house; since 1905 they had been committed to raising it to 16. Their attitude towards the raising of the age was supported by the great bulk of informed public opinion.

On 12th November 1946, in the debate on the Speech from the Throne the Prime Minister, Mr. C. R. Attlee, voiced the opinion of most thoughtful people in memorable words which echoed what W. E. Forster had said in 1870: 'We are straitened in our manpower. We must make up in quality what we lack in quantity. We are, therefore, raising the school leaving age.' Nevertheless, rumours persisted that the age would not be raised, until finally, on 17th January 1947, the Ministry of Education issued an authoritative statement that the school leaving age would definitely be raised, as arranged, on 1st April. To this resolve the Government adhered unflinchingly;

[1] The late Sir Hubert Henderson, in a letter to *The Times*, 26th February 1947.

even the disastrous spell of wintry weather in February and March, which exposed in all its nakedness the weakness of the country's economy, and held up building construction work of every kind for weeks, was not allowed to be sufficient cause for postponing the reform.

Whatever one's political views, it must be a matter of sincere regret that Miss Ellen Wilkinson, one of the most strenuous advocates of raising the age, did not live to see it accomplished. After months of agonizing fight against asthma, during which she continued to devote herself to her departmental duties with a heroism beyond praise, she died on 6th February 1947, at the early age of 56. She had literally worn herself out. Throughout her life, whatever the cause to which she gave herself, she gave without stint, and her fiery spirit proved in the end too much for her frail body.

Miss Wilkinson was succeeded as Minister of Education by Mr. George Tomlinson, who in his own inimitable way showed as keen an enthusiasm for educational reform as had his predecessor. A typical Lancashire man, with a rich sense of humour and an endless fund of witty stories, 'George', as everyone called him, endeared himself to every audience he addressed, and did much to popularize education, in the best sense of that term. His genuine desire to broaden and deepen opportunities for education sprang from a vivid sense of the loss he had himself sustained by having his own education cut short: he had left elementary school to enter a cotton mill at the age of 13. Unlike any previous head of the Education Department, he had had long experience of the local administration of education, having served as chairman of the education committee at Farnworth and as a member of the Lancashire education committee. In 1939 he was elected President of the Association of Education Committees. He brought also to the post of Minister of Education another valuable asset: an intimate knowledge of the current building situation, having been Minister of Works for the previous two years.

'George' used all these assets to the full during his considerable period of office, which lasted until the fall of the Labour Government in October 1951. What stature history will accord him remains to be seen, but there can be no doubt that he was 'the most popular Minister of Education that this country has ever known', and that 'he did not spare himself in his great task of implementing the Education Act of 1944.'[1] Over only one matter of policy, that of the age limit for taking the General Certificate of Education, did he fall foul of professional opinion: for the rest, he was invariably an encouraging and stimulating influence in the world of education, which lost a true friend and powerful supporter on his death in September 1952.

The raising of the school leaving age was accomplished in circumstances which, at best, could hardly be called propitious. What alone made it possible in 1947-8 was the fact that it was a gradual process, spread over an entire year. This was because the law allowed, and still allows, children to leave school at the end of the *term* (which includes the succeeding holiday), in which they reach the end of compulsory school age. So all those children who became 14 before 1st April 1947, were free to leave school then; and most did. The summer term of 1947 thus showed no increase in the total number of pupils in modern schools. In the autumn term those still aged 14 were retained, and so on until by September 1948 the entire age group was in the schools.

There were many circumstances which made the raising of the school leaving age in 1947 appear at the time 'an act of faith rather than an act of wisdom'. Apart from those enumerated above, the Government's building policy meant that the secondary modern schools could not expect buildings equipped for secondary work in place of the buildings designed for elementary work in which they were housed. That in itself was bound to prove a grave handicap—as indeed it has done—

[1] *Education*, 26th September 1952, p. 403.

to the development of genuine secondary education. Moreover, owing to the prevalent shortage of materials of all kinds, there was little likelihood that the schools would get much in the way of new equipment. But in my opinion the most serious cause for anxiety, though little note has ever been taken of this, was the fact that no systematic attempt on any large scale had been made to give the teachers in the modern schools advice or training to help them to face the tremendous problems involved in the change-over from elementary to secondary work.

This was no doubt in part due to the commendable English habit of not interfering with the teacher in the conduct of his professional duties and of throwing upon him the responsibility of working out his own school organization and curriculum. But it was also due to the fact that everyone in authority was much too busily occupied with the material side of reconstruction to pay much attention to the pedagogic. The result was that many modern school teachers assumed their new role with little idea of the immense issues involved and with but the vaguest notions of how to set about their new task.

It was not until 1947, more than two years after the official establishment of the modern school, and some months after the school leaving age had been raised, that the Ministry of Education issued anything approaching a comprehensive manual of guidance about secondary education. It is true that it had, in *The Nation's Schools* and *A Guide to the Educational System of England and Wales*, made some rather general observations about organization, curriculum and methods for modern schools. In *The Nation's Schools*, for example, the Ministry suggested[1] that 'free from the pressures of any external examination, these schools can work out the best and liveliest forms of secondary education suited to their pupils'. It had emphasized that there would be in modern schools 'a considerable number of children whose future employment will not demand any measure of technical skill or knowledge' and that these would present 'a

[1] p. 21.

definite educational problem'. It had assumed that 'a wide range of crafts would be developed'. It had warned that the standards of 'the more formal classroom studies . . . cannot be neglected or allowed to fall'. And it had advocated the use of 'projects'.

'Craft work is not the only form of practical activity which the senior school has been developing. What is commonly known as the 'project' has already proved its effectiveness in stimulating and maintaining interest in a way which the formal classroom lesson can not emulate.'[1]

That was perfectly true. Enterprising elementary schools had been experimenting with 'projects' ever since the early 1920s, and some astonishingly fine work had resulted. More work of the same high quality was produced by some modern schools after 1945. But the 'project' method is an exceedingly difficult one to handle effectively and unfortunately too many modern school teachers, not realizing this, and intoxicated by their new freedom, rushed ill-advisedly into an excess of 'projects', to the detriment of both discipline and standards of work.

Shortly before the age was raised the Ministry offered, in A.M. 208 (4th February 1947), advice on one very important point: the education of the 14–15-year-olds attending small rural 'all-age' schools. In these, as the Ministry pointed out, 'the older pupils cannot be taught in separate classes'; in other words, to give them genuinely secondary education was impossible. So, wherever it could be arranged, these children should, the Ministry suggested, be transferred to a neighbouring modern school.

If this were not feasible, the 14–15-year-olds from several schools might be concentrated at one of them, so as to form a class of their own. If even this could not be done, then perhaps additional use might be made of the district centres for practical instruction which many authorities had established in rural

[1] p. 22.

parts of their areas. In this case, as the children would spend only part of the week in the centre and the rest in their own schools, the Ministry suggested that the work at the centres might be organized on 'project' lines and children given individual or group tasks which they could continue at their schools.

Further suggestions made in the memorandum were that peripatetic specialist teachers might be sent round the small schools, possibly 'provided with a van containing a film projector, a wireless set, and a radiogram, as well as apparatus for various educational activities'; and that the 14–15-year-olds might be grouped in a camp school or a school with boarding facilities for residential courses of a month or two at a time.

The expedient most frequently adopted was that of transferring the 'additional year' to a properly organized modern school. Where this procedure was handled intelligently and sympathetically by the head teacher of the modern school, as it often was, it had most beneficial results. I visited one Yorkshire girls' school, for example, where the transferred pupils, drawn from some twenty small schools, not only had the advantage of the modern school's domestic science and other practical rooms, but were also kept in touch with their villages by being given the task of making a social survey of them. In the course of this they learned much more about their home neighbourhood than they had ever known before! Nor were the benefits of this scheme confined to the transferred pupils; the town girls, who participated in the survey, got to know the surrounding countryside, and the grown-ups in the villages became keenly interested in the work of the town school.

But all these devices were, after all, only temporary expedients which could rarely, if ever, be wholly satisfactory. The only way to make it possible for all children to enjoy a genuinely secondary education is to eliminate the 'all-age' school and to provide properly equipped secondary schools. Throughout the period under review the Government's policy precluded the replacement of old school buildings by new. No building was permitted for purposes of 'reorganization'. Yet somehow the local education authorities had managed by January 1952 to reduce the number of 'all-age' schools from the 8,800 of 1945 to 5,107, and the number of pupils being taught in such schools by about one-quarter: in the circumstances no slight achievement. Yet at that rate it would still take a further twenty years or more to do away altogether with the 'all-age' school.

In *The New Secondary Education*,[1] published in 1947, the Ministry of Education attempted something like a comprehensive survey of the parts which in its opinion the three main types of secondary schools should play. The twenty pages devoted to the modern school still repay careful study, though as early as 1952 it had begun to appear that the main lines of modern school development might diverge in important particulars from those proposed in this 1947 pamphlet.

This was only as was expected, indeed encouraged. Miss Ellen Wilkinson concluded the Foreword she wrote to the Pamphlet (which was published after her death) with these words:[2]

'It is important not to make plans that are too rigid . . . The schools must have freedom to experiment, room to grow, variety for the sake of freshness, for the fun of it even. Laughter in the classroom, self-confidence growing every day, eager interest instead of bored uniformity, this is the way to produce from our fine stock the Britons who will have no need to fear the new scientific age, but will stride into it, heads high, determined to master science and to serve mankind.'

It is no exaggeration to say that the good modern schools—and there are many of them—have lived up to the spirit of those words.

In a chapter entitled 'Different Types of Secondary Education'[3] the Ministry made the following observations about modern school education and the modern school:

[1] Ministry of Education Pamphlet No. 9. H.M. Stationery Office, 1947.
[2] p. 5.   [3] Chapter V, pp. 22–5. The quotation is from p. 23.

'Experience has shown that the majority of children learn most easily by dealing with concrete things and following a course rooted in their own day-to-day experience. At the age of 11 few of them will have disclosed particular interests and aptitudes well enough marked for them to require any other course. The majority will do best in a *school which provides a good all-round education in an atmosphere which enables them to develop freely along their own lines. Such a school will give them a chance to sample a variety of 'subjects' and skills and to pursue those which attract them most. It is for this majority that the secondary modern school will cater.*' (Italics mine.)

In the chapter[1] devoted to 'Modern School Education', the following general statement of the aims of the modern school was given:

'The aim of the modern school is to provide a good all-round secondary education, not focused primarily on the traditional subjects of the school curriculum, but developing out of the interests of the children. Through its appeal to their interests it will stimulate their ability to learn and will teach them to pursue quality in thought, expression and craftsmanship. It will interpret the modern world to them and give them a preparation for life in the widest sense, including a full use of leisure. It will aim at getting the most out of every pupil that he is capable of, at making him adaptable, and at teaching him to do a job properly, and thoroughly and not to be satisfied with bad workmanship, and to be exact in what he says and does.'

Three fundamental ideas appear to underlie these passages. First, that education in the modern school should be based on activity and experience rather than on academic study. Second, that the education should be largely unspecialized, though by way of 'sampling' pupils would arrive at the subjects and skills 'which attract them most'. Thirdly, that the education would be unsystematic, in the conventional pedagogic sense of that term, that is, 'not focused on the traditional subjects of

[1] Chapter VII, pp. 28–47. Quotation from pp. 29–30.

the school curriculum, but developing out of the interests of the children', though systematic in its search for dominant interests and in the pursuit through them of knowledge, skill and desirable qualities of character. The teacher's task envisaged—if this analysis be correct—was thus both novel and of immense difficulty. It is hardly surprising that, during the years under review, most modern schools came to prefer somewhat easier routes, to which indeed they were often directed by both their own judgement and external demands upon the schools.

A few pages later[1] the Ministry went into some detail about the curriculum. Its suggestions here appeared at first sight to run contrary to the foregoing for it assumed that among the subjects which would be taught in all modern schools would be, on the academic side English (and Welsh in Wales), mathematics, history, geography and science, and on the practical, physical education, art, music, handicrafts, housecraft and, where possible, gardening and animal husbandry. In many schools, it was suggested, a foreign language would be taught; and this was definitely encouraged. 'Children who have a taste for it and whose attainments in English suggest that they have some linguistic ability should have an opportunity to learn a foreign language . . .'

But these suggestions, it was explained, were for guidance only. In modern schools, as in all others, religious education would be compulsory; but apart from that, 'Neither the subjects of the curriculum, nor the time spent on each, nor the way they are to be taught is laid down by the Ministry of Education.' The responsibility in these matters lay with the head of the school; and once again the heads of modern schools were encouraged to experiment freely. 'Freedom and flexibility are of its [the modern school's] essence and are indeed its great opportunity.'

In handling the academic subjects teachers were advised

[1] pp. 34–42.

to take a practical and realistic approach. In the teaching of history and geography, for example, the value of making local surveys was emphasized. In mathematics, 'The best schools relate the subject to the needs of practical life' and introduce 'those forms of mathematical expression of which the ordinary citizen requires some understanding if he takes an interest in the world of the air age, with its machines, its statistics and its increasing use of a mathematically based vocabulary.' In biology, 'Topics for study should be selected for their intrinsic importance and interest and not because they fall within certain conventional branches of the subject.' If a foreign language were taught, 'oral work will predominate, and the aim must be to attain the ability to use and understand a living language, not to study it as if it were a dead one.'

In a shorter section[1] the aims and functions of the practical subjects were briefly reviewed. It was suggested that these had much value as intellectual training; music, it was said, was a superb example of this, while 'the so-called practical subjects . . . give a training in accuracy and in planning a job in advance, a sense of standards, and a discipline that are an essential part of the intellectual process.' The chief aim of education in arts and crafts was 'to help children to be actively aware of and to enjoy beauty in nature and in art, and to appreciate fine and honest craftsmanship wherever they see it.' Art and craft should be 'primarily approached . . . through the children's own creative experiments in as many materials as possible.'

In a longer passage[2] the Ministry again advocated the 'project' method as 'one of the most promising lines of solution in the modern school.' It was claimed that, 'if properly handled', this method could 'certainly offer as good a chance of a sound intellectual training as any other', and could also 'help in the social training given by the school'. But the authors of the pamphlet warned teachers that: 'It is not easy to bring off

[1] pp. 41–2.   [2] pp. 38–41.

successfully. It demands [of the teachers] a rather special measure of imagination and mental alertness.' It is a pity that more heed was not paid to this warning, which might with advantage have been more specific.

The use of 'project' and similar methods raised an issue of fundamental importance. Was education in the modern school to be conceived in terms of systematic and progressive instruction or not? The advice given by the Ministry seemed to suggest that on the whole it was not. It is difficult to put any other interpretation on the phrase 'not focused primarily on the traditional subjects of the school curriculum but developing out of the interests of the children', especially when this is linked with persistent advocacy of 'projects'. For it is not possible to give systematic and progressive instruction during the course of a 'project', but only in time separately allotted. Unfortunately the Ministry did not raise this point, and many teachers at first overlooked it. Most of them, to their credit, quickly realized it, but others did not until much damage to pupils' progress had been done, and public outcry raised over waste of time and gaps in the knowledge—especially of the 3 R's—of children coming out of the modern school.

All things considered, *The New Secondary Education* was a valuable guide to the modern school teacher, and I know that many teachers profited from it. Had it been issued a couple of years earlier it would have been far more valuable. By the time it appeared modern school teachers were heavily engaged in the opening struggles of their great new venture, and many, I know, were too preoccupied with immediate tasks to give the pamphlet the attention they were well aware it deserved. Far too many others, unfortunately, did not trouble even to read it.

The first main task before the modern schools in 1947–8 was to make the 'extra year' worth while for the older pupils retained in school. Happily, except in a few districts, mainly industrial, where the tradition of early employment was strong and vacancies for young workers were numerous, there was very little hostility, from either parents or employers, to the raising of the school age. This gave the schools a good start, and while many failed to take full advantage of their opportunity there is abundant evidence that many seized it with both hands.

On 12th June 1948, a special correspondent of *The Times Educational Supplement*, who had made a series of visits to modern schools of all kinds, wrote as follows:

'The new 14–15 age group is getting a much better chance than at one time seemed possible. The suggestion that the pupils in this age group are wasting their time is not true. A great effort has been made by nearly all authorities to plan suitable courses for them, and although in some unreorganized schools it is difficult to do much more than consolidate what already is expected to be known, even here something is added to knowledge and a wider horizon shown. In the good new secondary modern schools the gain is immense.'

On 30th September 1948, the *Schoolmaster*, the official journal of the National Union of Teachers, stated in a leading article that:

'The local Press in many parts of the country has been commenting upon the results of the first full year of the working of the higher school-leaving age. It can be said straight away that the comments have been universally favourable. There have been no adverse criticisms of the children or of the reform itself; on the contrary, much benefit has been discovered, of a character calculated to encourage teachers and to justify the faith of those who worked for the reform through so many years. Reports from all quarters say that the children are more mature in mind and body, have a greater sense of responsibility, and have benefited in physique and character.'

In its annual Report for 1948[1] the Ministry of Education summed up the results of the first year as follows:

[1] *Education in 1948*. H.M. Stationery Office, 1949, pp. 9–10.

'On the whole, the picture is encouraging. In a few areas, and in a few individual schools elsewhere, the extra year was a striking success. In the majority of schools it was clearly worth while.'

The Ministry pointed out that most schools were hampered by 'inherited or current' shortages, but added (what every teacher knows) that 'the success or failure of the extra year depended in each school more on the quality of the head and assistant staff than on all the other factors combined.'

'Wherever the teachers showed energy and initiative in providing for the older children the year was a success whatever the material obstacles. Where these qualities were lacking, the year was largely wasted and the children themselves were resentful and frustrated.'

As might be expected, on the whole the new régime was more successful in the modern schools proper (i.e., those separately organized) than in the unreorganized 'all-age' schools. In the former 'there was little difficulty in absorbing the extra age group', and 'where local education authorities and teachers had thought about the problems in advance, they were able to replan the work of the whole school so that the extra year was not artificially added to an existing course, but was, as it should be, the fourth year of a four-year course'. In the 'all-age' schools 'In general . . . less was done to meet the special needs of the older children, and though there were many notable exceptions, the year was of value more as showing the problems to be solved in the future than for achievement.'

Some idea of what the chief among these problems would be had been given in *The New Secondary Education*. 'Perhaps the main difference between a modern school and other types of secondary schools', this observed,[1] 'is its very broad outlook and objective.'

'It has to provide a series of courses for children of widely differing ability, aptitude and social background. It has to

---
[1] p. 29.

cater for the needs of intelligent boys and girls, for those with a marked practical bent, as well as for the special problem of the backward children.'

It is perhaps even yet not generally realized how wide the range of ability can be within a single modern school, or even class. An extreme instance of the latter was given in 1952 by Miss L. A. Howland, in a lecture at the London University Institute of Education. She told of 'one set of fourth-year pupils which included two girls who were working for entrance to the Royal Academy of Music, one who was hoping to get into the Royal Academy of Dramatic Art, four who wanted to become teachers, three taking a pre-nursing course, and, by contrast, one schizophrenic, one epileptic, and several who could neither read nor write'.[1] It was certainly exceptional to find such a range within a single class, but it could be paralleled in many a modern school.

Because of this very wide range of mental ability, the pamphlet had suggested[2] that 'it is on the side of intellectual training that the biggest differences will be found between the modern school and other types of secondary school'. That not all modern schools were at first successful in coping with this particular problem is clear from the Ministry's Report for 1949,[3] in which an assessment, based on notes by H.M. Inspectors, was attempted of the quality of the education being given in primary and secondary schools. A single sentence in that Report[4] epitomizes the tributes paid to and the criticisms made of the modern schools at the time.

'If many modern schools are now human, civilizing places with much to offer to the social and spiritual side of their pupils' development, far fewer seem to have come to grips with the problems of how to meet intellectual needs and how to stimulate fullest effort.'

This criticism was, I think, a fair one, though, as I had reason

[1] *Schoolmaster*, 31.x.52. p. 479.   [2] p. 34.
[3] *Education in 1949*. H.M. Stationery Office, 1950.   [4] p. 23.

to know at first-hand from the fairly frequent visits I was paying to modern schools, there were many notable exceptions to the general rule.

There were, I think, two main reasons why the modern school was during these first three years of its existence so singularly successful in developing social virtues and so much less successful in stimulating intellectual effort and maintaining academic standards. The first had its roots way back in days long before 1945.

From at least as early as the publication of the Hadow Report in 1926 the senior elementary schools had had it dinned into them that they were dealing with practically-minded pupils. Their business, they were told, was to get away from sole, or main, reliance on academic studies. From 1943 onwards emphasis on the 'non-bookish' aspect of modern secondary education was redoubled. The modern schools were adjured, even implored, from innumerable public platforms and in innumerable Press articles, not to become 'pale shadows of the grammar school'. It is hardly to be wondered at that many modern school teachers, exhilarated by the concurrent exhortations to experiment largely and freely, took their mentors at their word. It is no more to be wondered at that some went rather to extremes in 'deintellectualizing' the content of the education they gave their pupils.

In particular, following the Ministry's advice, which was reiterated by many of His Majesty's Inspectors on their routine visits to schools, numerous teachers set out to organize their entire school curriculum on 'project', 'centre of interest' or similar lines. Now, as has been previously noted, unless these methods are very skilfully handled, they inevitably result in patchy knowledge and unsystematic habits of work. That was unfortunately what happened in too many cases. Some teachers who embarked on 'projects' neither understood nor were interested, nor believed in the method; they undertook it because the head of the school wanted them to or H.M.I. had urged it on them. Others were enthusiastic enough—perhaps too enthusiastic—but had not the grip to control it in practice nor the judgement to set it in its proper place in school life.

It must be emphasized, however, that there were instances in which teachers organized the work of schools or classes along these lines with striking success. Their pupils not only produced work, including academic work, of very high standard,' but acquired accurate and systematic knowledge over a much broader field than would have been possible by sole reliance upon straight class teaching. I saw several cases. I remember particularly one girls' school in Yorkshire—housed in shocking premises—where the work of the entire school had been organized in a series of four progressive projects each lasting a year: 'Ourselves and our homes', 'Ourselves and our districts', 'Ourselves and our country', 'Ourselves and our world'. The work was brilliant, its range immense, and its academic standard as high, age for age, as that in many grammar schools. I could cite other instances from my own experience; and readers who visited the Schools' section at the Festival of Britain will recall the quality and range of the work in the projects exhibited there.

The second reason for the low standard of academic work found in many schools in 1948 was a very different one. *The New Secondary Education* had warned teachers of the problem which the presence in modern schools of many dull and retarded children would present, and had admitted that these would include educationally sub-normal children who ought properly to be in special schools. This was not, of course, a new problem; the senior elementary school had always had to cope with it. But the lengthening of the school course, the concentration of 14–15-year-olds from small schools (where often standards were low) in larger ones, the after-effects of war, and the abolition of fees in maintained secondary schools (which meant that parents could no longer get dull children into grammar schools by paying for them, while all the brighter children now went automatically to these schools), together with, I feel sure, an expectation of a higher standard of work from the modern than from the senior elementary school, all contributed to make the problem bulk larger and more obvious.

It is a grave defect in our educational system that hardly any teachers are specifically trained to handle dull or backward—as distinct from educationally sub-normal—children:[1] work which demands specialist qualifications as well as exceptional personal qualities. As a result, in many modern schools the special treatment which such children require could not be arranged. In schools where 'project' or 'centre of interest' work predominated, some of these children did little or no intellectual work; it was easier to employ them principally on the manual jobs which 'projects' and similar activities can always supply. This was no doubt thoroughly good for them in many ways, but in a highly civilized society literacy is a necessity for all adults; and many of these children were being allowed to leave school barely if at all literate.

Three or four years later a very different state of affairs was to be found in modern schools. During my 1952 survey I could not fail to be struck by three marked changes: first, a notably greater attention to the '3 Rs' in particular and to academic studies in general; second, a pronounced swing away from 'projects' as a main feature in the curriculum; and third, a greatly increased provision of vocationally biased courses during the latter half of the school programme. Moreover, whatever the organization or method, the schools' work was everywhere firmer and more balanced. I must add that the schools I visited were, with few exceptions, among the best in their areas.

A number of local authorities had already stereotyped the biased course pattern throughout their areas, and others were

[1] This was still unhappily true in 1952. Only one training course of any length was available; and this (at the London University Institute of Education) was limited to thirty members a year. Other courses were, however, projected.

in process of doing so. Southampton, for example, was offering in its sixteen modern schools a choice of five biased courses for boys and four for girls. This included two (one for boys and one for girls) called 'General', in which pupils were prepared for the General Certificate of Education. The others were 'Craftsmanship' (two courses, one biased towards engineering, the other towards art); 'Secretarial' (for girls); 'Art and Crafts' (for children of lesser intellectual ability); and 'Seamanship'. This authority was also proposing to include a school with an agricultural bias.

Portsmouth was offering to girls a choice of six 'Advanced Courses', in domestic science, catering, pre-nursing, art, commerce, and academic studies. This last, like the Southampton 'General' course, was a specific preparation for G.C.E. Croydon, which was proposing to divide its area into four districts and to offer in each no fewer than ten biased courses, similarly included one termed 'less rigorous academic'. Northumberland, on the other hand, a predominantly rural area, was in process of establishing six schools all offering an agricultural course. These Northumberland schools were, incidentally, to be provided with hostels for boarders—a practice which was spreading in rural countries by 1952.

Most authorities still felt, however, that the time had not yet come for any such hard and fast arrangements, and were encouraging their schools to develop as seemed best in their particular circumstances. Consequently, one found the widest variety of growths. This ranged in my new experience from a school with a selective entry—'an overlap between the grammar, technical and modern schools', as the head described it—which was running a five-year course and entering its fifth year pupils *en bloc* for the G.C.E., to the school which transferred some 10 per cent of its abler pupils at the end of two years to grammar and technical schools and was spending much of its time and energy on remedial work in the 3 Rs with its many children of low-grade intellectual ability.

The presence in considerable numbers of such children constituted a serious problem in several of the schools I visited. But the problem which was exercising the minds of modern school teachers far more was that of the children at the other end of the intelligence scale: those who had failed by a narrow margin to get into grammar schools. This was partly because almost everywhere, but especially in large towns, the schools were under heavy pressure from parents of such children to get them transferred. But it was due also to a very general feeling of unease among modern school teachers that these children were not getting a fair deal. Parental pressure was undoubtedly responsible in part—possibly in large part—for the increased attention to academic studies in many modern schools, and especially for the growing practice of entering pupils for the G.C.E. and other external examinations. But it would be quite wrong to assume that it was the only cause. There can be no doubt that the desire of teachers to give their pupils as good a chance as possible in after life was largely responsible. They were as well aware as any parents that so long as the modern school concentrated wholly upon 'practical' activities and eschewed examinations in academic subjects, so long would its pupils be virtually prevented from entering professional and semi-professional occupations. And they realized that among their abler pupils there were some at least who were not only fitted to enter such occupations but for whom a more academic course than had been generally envisaged for the modern school was the most suitable. It is not only the most intellectually able children who are fond of books and 'bookish' subjects: apart from any innate predispositions which may exist, there are many homes of no great intellectual capacity where, owing to the parents' tastes or occupations (or both) children grow up in an atmosphere which gives them an academic rather than a 'practical' attitude to life and employment.

But there was also another factor influencing this return to academic studies and their concomitant, external examinations. I found widespread among modern school teachers a longing for some recognized 'yardstick' by which they could measure the standard of their work. 'We were delighted when we were told we should be free from examinations', one head said to me, 'but now we are wondering what on earth to put in their place'. I was told that the children had the same desire: 'even when they are happy and are making progress they still feel the need to know they are achieving some standard.' In practical activities they could judge by the products they made; in academic studies they felt at a loss.

If there were some such 'yardstick', teachers felt also, most of the antagonism towards the modern school exhibited by ambitious parents would disappear. That such antagonism still persisted in 1952 in many places was unquestionable, though it was equally certainly confined to the relatively small minority of parents who were disappointed because their children had not got to the grammar school. Many even among such parents, I was frequently assured, got over their disappointment when they discovered how well the modern school was suiting their children. But they got over it most quickly and completely when they found that the school offered pupils the chance of taking G.C.E.

It is certain that on the whole the prestige of the modern school rose steadily, and in places rapidly, during these years. Here and there an exceptionally good modern school—usually though not always one possessing fine up-to-date buildings and extensive playing fields—was held in better repute by most parents than the grammar school. Such instances were still rare, but there were many modern schools which were already secure in the esteem of their neighbourhoods and confident in their ability to do a good job by the children who came to them.

EXPERIMENT IN SECONDARY EDUCATION

TRANSFER BETWEEN SCHOOLS

That job, they considered, included securing transfers for children whom they thought would do well in a grammar school. The last seven words in that sentence are important. From the moment the tripartite organization of secondary education entered the field of practical politics it was taken for granted that children found to be unsuited to the type of education they were receiving, that is, in blunter language, children who were misfits, would be transferred to another. But during these years modern school teachers considerably broadened the basis of transfer by freely recommending for it, not only misfits but, in very much larger numbers, children who were both happy and successful in a modern school. (One paradoxical consequence of this was that in some schools children were refusing transfers.)

The concept of transfer was also broadened in another way. The original intention had been that most transfers would take place after two years in secondary school. But during these years there quickly developed a much more flexible system than that. I found in 1952 transfers being made at all stages from the end of a child's first term at secondary school to the end of a five-year course. Probably the majority of transfers were still being made at the end of the second year, but by 1952 it would have been rash to say that this was the rule.

One of the most interesting types of transfer was that by which children went after a five-year course at a modern school into the sixth form of a grammar school. There were by 1952 already cases of pupils who had entered the university by this route. In other places—Devon, for example—children were being accepted direct from the modern school course into full-time courses at Colleges of Further Education. This latter idea was attracting a number of local authorities: Southend-on-Sea, for example, was intending to close its technical secondary school and to provide in its modern schools 'end-on' courses leading to further courses at its municipal college.

To my mind, the least satisfactory form of transfer operating in 1952 was that based on an examination held in all modern schools throughout a local authority's area at the end of the second year of secondary school, with all children who passed this being given the opportunity to transfer to a technical or grammar school. This method seemed to me designed to weaken the modern school without much likelihood of strengthening the others. Where such transfers were at all numerous they had a devastating effect on the denuded modern schools. As one head put it to me; 'the better the lower part of my school the worse the top'. The effect upon morale can be imagined.

This head went on to explain that he would not mind so much if he felt that the children who transferred were fully capable of standing up to the more rigorous academic courses of the grammar and technical schools. But in his opinion most of them were not. He expressed a very general feeling among modern school teachers when he declared this to be the main weakness of the transfer system.

I cannot agree that this was the main weakness. To my mind, this was that nearly all transfers were one-way: 'upward', from modern to grammar or (much less frequently) technical school. It was still in 1952 extremely rare to find a two-way system operating on a basis of equality. That children were being transferred from modern to other types of secondary schools who were, to say the least, unlikely to stay the course seemed to me highly dangerous. But I regarded as even more dangerous the fact that children in grammar schools who were manifestly unequal to the intellectual demands of grammar school work were *not* being transferred. Of all types of secondary schools the grammar school can least afford to carry passengers, and in no other type of school are the penalties for failure, in terms both of material prospects and personal frustration, so severe. For reasons given on previous pages it would not have been logical to expect as many transfers from as into the grammar school. But the transfer system was suggesting that almost none were needed. The opinions of grammar school teachers, the numerous early withdrawals (not by any means all for economic reasons), and the high failure rate in the School Certificate and General Certificate examinations offered strong evidence against this hypothesis.

GRAMMAR SCHOOL MISGIVINGS

The story of the grammar school during these years is not an altogether happy one. There was from the start widespread fear among grammar school teachers that there was implicit in the provisions of the Education Act, 1944, the threat of a 'levelling down' of grammar school standards. Such passages as the following, from the May 1945 number of the *A.M.A.*,[1] the official journal of the Incorporated Association of Assistant Masters in Secondary Schools, became common currency among them:

'The Association has of late been much concerned to see to it that the so-called equality [i.e., of all types of secondary schools] is not attained by levelling down and by putting a premium on mediocrity. If full educational opportunities are denied to able children whose parents cannot afford to send them to fee-paying schools, we may indeed get equality throughout the State system, but it will not be based on equity, and national efficiency will suffer.'

There were three points at which the grammar school felt especially threatened: in its freedom to govern itself, its right to choose its pupils, and the salaries paid from 1945 on to its teachers. As early as 1944 and 1945 a series of events seemed to give substance to fears on all these three counts.

In March 1945 the Ministry of Education issued a Code of Regulations applicable to all primary and secondary schools;

[1] Editorial Comment, p. 93.

many grammar school teachers found in these 'rules more suitable for senior elementary schools', as one of them put it. The requirement made by Regulation 20 that the school year was to amount to 'a period of not less than forty weeks during which the school shall meet on not less than two hundred days' was particularly resented, for it meant a general reduction by about two weeks of grammar school holidays. This led to widespread and bitter complaints which re-echoed through the Press for years.

But it was the Regulations made for Direct Grant grammar schools which provoked the deepest fears. The maintained grammar schools had throughout the whole period of their existence looked to the independent 'Public' schools for their standards, of both conduct and academic attainment, and had regarded the Direct Grant grammar schools as a 'bridge' between themselves and the independent schools. The Direct Grant schools were within the State system, in that they received grants from public funds, yet they retained a measure of freedom comparable with that of the independent schools. To attain to such freedom was a cherished ambition of many heads of maintained grammar schools: either by securing a place on the Direct Grant list or by sharing in a general extension to maintained schools of the freedom accorded to those on Direct Grant.

The fears aroused by the new Regulations for the Direct Grant schools were ambivalent. On the one hand the permission accorded to the Direct Grant schools to continue to charge tuition fees, even if on a restricted basis, put this group of schools on quite a different footing from the maintained schools, in which all places were to be free. On the other, various alterations in the conditions of grant to Direct Grant schools appeared seriously to curtail their freedom. The withdrawal of grant from their preparatory and junior divisions, the condition that 'the minimum educational standard qualifying the pupil for admission to or retention in the school shall be the

EXPERIMENT IN SECONDARY EDUCATION

same for all pupils of similar age', the addition of 'reserved' to free places (which in effect reduced the governors' right to select their pupils to 50 per cent of the entry) and the control by the Ministry of the rate of tuition fees which might be charged, all tended towards this effect. The new conditions were, in fact, felt to be so intolerable by some thirty schools on the Direct Grant list that they withdrew from it and became independent.

This was for many grammar school teachers the writing on the wall. If Direct Grant schools felt that so much freedom was being taken from them that they must escape from State control, to what degree of bondage might the maintained schools not expect to be subject? They were openly threatened with the loss of their individual governing bodies by the provision in the Act that a local education authority could 'make an arrangement for the constitution of a single governing body for any two or more county schools or voluntary schools . . .' As illustration of the lengths to which this might be carried the story was widely circulated in 1945 of a county borough which had deprived a grammar school of its governing body simply because it was unable to find enough people to form governing bodies for its modern schools.

Moreover, under the new régime, pupils were to be allocated to secondary schools by the local education authority, which meant, argued the grammar schools, that heads would no longer have any say in selecting their entrants. And assistant teachers were to be appointed to the service of the Authority, not to individual schools. Visions of being moved about like a pawn on a chessboard disturbed the sleep of many a grammar school teacher during the early days after 1944.

The 1945 salary scales came as a sharp humiliation to the grammar school. There had always been previously, ever since the introduction of the Burnham Scales in 1919, different scales of salaries for secondary and elementary school teachers; and the former had always been substantially higher than the latter. Now, to their shocked surprise, grammar school teachers found themselves placed on the same basic scale, and given, by way of additional allowances, what seemed to them totally inadequate financial recognition of their superior academic qualifications and the difficult and responsible nature of their work.

As noted in Chapter Two,[1] the representatives of the grammar school on the teachers' panel of the Burnham Committee strove their utmost to secure a substantial additional allowance over and above the basic scale for an assistant teacher in possession of a university degree. The basis of their argument was that:

'... the secondary [i.e., the grammar] school scales must be so designed that the schools will attract to the service an adequate number of trained teachers who are graduates or who hold equivalent qualifications. This can only be achieved if the scales offer assured incomes comparable with the rewards that may be obtained in other professions by men and women of like ability and resource ...'[2]

The scale which the Assistant Masters' Association proposed for graduate male assistants was £400 a year rising by annual increments of £30 to £800, with an additional allowance of £50 a year for each year of training beyond the minimum of two years. They asked also for special responsibility allowances of £100 a year for senior masters and £50 a year for heads of departments. As a three-year university degree course followed by one year in a University Training Department counted as four years of training for a teacher, this would have meant that a male graduate assistant teacher would have started his career with a salary of £500.

These demands seemed much too modest to many grammar school teachers. But they were rejected by the Burnham Committee. The possession of a degree was held to merit an allowance of only £15 a year for men and £12 a year for women at the minimum of the scale and twice as much at the maximum. Each additional year of training beyond two carried a similar allowance. A graduate male assistant teacher thus began on a

[1] p. 34.   [2] *A.M.A.* November-December 1944, p. 197.

salary of £345. The unkindest blow dealt to grammar school teachers by the Burnham Committee was the ruling that if an assistant teacher received an allowance in respect of a post of special responsibility he lost the allowance for a degree. This was, it must be said, a piece of indefensible meanness.

The representatives of the grammar school felt keenly that their case had been insufficiently supported by the representatives of the National Union of Teachers—which held sixteen of the twenty-six seats on the Teachers' Panel and whose opinion was therefore decisive. So aggrieved were they about this that they took the unprecedented step of dissenting in the full Burnham Committee from the decision taken by the Teachers' Panel to accept the offer made by the Authorities' Panel.

This action provoked great indignation among members of the N.U.T.—not without reason, for it threatened to destroy the basis upon which negotiations were conducted in the Burnham Committee. It had long been the accepted procedure that the panels should confer separately until they had reached an agreed decision, and that when they met in full committee only the leaders of the respective panels should speak. This being so, the action taken by the grammar school representatives seems inexcusable, though in their defence it must be said that when the secondary associations had agreed, reluctantly, to accept representation on the reconstituted Burnham Committee[1] they had stated in writing that:

'Since the proposed reconstitution and suggested procedure apparently afford no opportunity for the expression of minority views through the machinery of the Burnham Committee, our constituent Associations will undoubtedly feel that they must reserve the right to use other means of making their opinions known.'[2]

---

[1] The previous separate committees for elementary and secondary school teachers had been amalgamated to form a single committee for primary and secondary teachers.

[2] Quoted from the *A.M.A.* January–February 1945, p. 40.

The grammar school representatives did not rest content with voicing their dissatisfaction in the Burnham Committee. They canvassed Parliamentary and public opinion vigorously, and were successful, not only in securing numerous letters to the Press in support of their demands, but also in getting the matter debated in the House of Commons. Here, on 20th February 1945, Mr. Kenneth Lindsay stated their case forcefully:

'What are these secondary schools and who are the teachers? There are some 1,100 maintained and aided secondary schools in the country . . . They are not privileged schools. Forty-six per cent of their pupils pay no fees and 70 per cent of their new entrants will have earned "special places". They are the only schools in this country which for some years ahead will give full-time education up to and beyond 16. They provide more than half the open scholarships and exhibitions to Oxford and Cambridge. Two-thirds of the winners of these scholarships have not paid fees and were previously educated at elementary schools . . .

'If there are high standards among our scientists and our scholars and our civil servants, to whom is this due? . . . to the devoted men and women, inspired scholars, who gave up a lifetime in and out of school, in long hours of correcting homework, in school societies and a score of outside activities, and it is these men and women who have trained themselves, who have sacrificed three or four years at the university . . . who in the future are to receive £15 or £12 if they are women—for their trouble.'[1]

That put the case in a nutshell—or, rather, it put the better of the two cases the grammar school seemed concerned to defend. The *Journal of Education* was not altogether beside the mark when it wrote[2] that 'They have too often seemed to value most highly those prerogatives such as the retention of fees which carried with them implications of social superiority, instead of welcoming as their distinctive and supremely im-

[1] *ibid.*, p. 64.   [2] Editorial comment, September 1945.

portant function the education of boys and girls of superior academic ability . . .' Later, the latter became increasingly the foundation on which the grammar school case was based.

It was not only the assistant teachers in the grammar school who were shocked by the 1945 Burnham scales; heads received an even more shattering blow. Hitherto their salaries had been outside the scales; they had been a matter of local or individual agreement. But in the 1945 Burnham Agreement they found themselves, like everybody else, placed on the basic scale, and treated merely as teachers holding posts of special responsibility. The additional allowances accruing to them were based on the numbers of pupils in their schools, which were ranked in the following five grades:

Grade I	Not over 100 on roll
Grade II	Over 100 but not over 200
Grade III	Over 200 but not over 350
Grade IV	Over 350 but not over 500
Grade V	Over 500 on roll.

The respective allowances were 2, 4, 6, 8, or 10 increments, of £15 a year for men or £12 for women.

Many heads felt this method of payment to be derogatory to their dignity. But that was not all; it meant also a considerable reduction in the value of many posts (though the salaries of their present holders were not to be reduced), despite a clause which benefited grammar school heads almost exclusively.

'When a school contains not fewer than 30 pupils who have attained the age of 15 years, there shall be added to the salary payable to the Head Teacher . . . a sum of £50 (men) and £40 (women) in respect of each unit of 30 such pupils, provided that where the number of such pupils exceeds 30 or a multiple of 30 by 16 or more, it shall be treated . . . as if it were the next higher multiple of 30.'[1]

[1] *Report of the Burnham Committee*, 1945. H.M. Stationery Office, para. 5(b).

Very few secondary schools other than grammar schools qualified in 1945, or seemed likely to qualify in the near future, for a head teacher's allowance of any size under that clause. Yet even this arrangement was a cause for complaint. Grammar school heads objected, justifiably, that it exposed them to the temptation to induce boys and girls to remain at school irrespective of whether or not it was educationally profitable for them to do so. It meant also that the head's salary would be a fluctuating one, for the allowance was to be assessed, and consequently adjusted, annually. As the assessment for any forthcoming year was to be based on the number of pupils of 15 and upwards on roll in March of the preceding year, it can be seen that a head was placed in a most invidious position when called upon to advise parents whether older boys or girls should remain another year at school.

The demerits of this scheme for adding to the head's salary were not removed by the introduction in 1948, when another Burnham Agreement came into force, of a different, and more elaborate, method of assessment. Under this schools were ranked in no fewer than twenty-three categories, on the basis of what was called the 'unit total'. Instead of reckoning the crude number of pupils of age 15 and upwards in a school, pupils were given a value in points, or 'units', according to their ages: a pupil under the age of 15 counted as one unit, a pupil aged 15 as four units, of 16 seven, and of 17 or over ten. The scale of allowances ranged from £55 (men) or £50 (women) for a school of up to forty units to £900 (men) or £790 (women) for a school of 300 units or more.

The battle for substantially larger additional allowances for grammar school teachers continued without abatement throughout the years under review. By 1951 the grammar school representatives had won at least a partial victory, for they had succeeded in pushing up the graduate allowance to £60 a year (men) and £48 (women). They may also be considered to have gained a further victory in the 1951 scales by the introduction of a much more flexible system for the payment of allowances for special responsibility.

In 1945 such posts were to be 15 per cent of the total number of qualified assistant teachers in the service of a local education authority, and they were to carry allowances ranging from £50 to £100 a year (men), or £40 to £80 (women). In 1951 both the percentage of places and the upper limits on the amount that might be paid were discontinued. Both were left to the discretion of the local authority, subject to the following conditions:

(i) no allowance was to be less than £40 a year.

(ii) every school with a unit total exceeding a hundred was to carry such posts, which were to be paid within a prescribed range of expenditure, as under:

> For unit totals between 101 and 200   £40 to £50
> For unit totals between 201 and 250   £40 to £60
> For unit totals between 251 and 350   £40 to £100
> For unit totals between 351 and 400   £80 to £120

Thereafter, for each 100 units there were to be further allowances on a progressive scale; for example, for each 100 units between 401 and 700 a sum between £50 and £75 was to be added, for each 100 units over 2,000 a sum between £100 and £150.

It was mandatory upon the authorities to pay these amounts. In addition there was created an 'Area Pool' for each authority, calculated at the rate of four shillings a head for each pupil on the registers of the primary, secondary and special schools maintained by the authority. The money in this pool could be used by the authority for the following purposes:

(i) to pay increased allowances, or additional allowances, to assistant teachers involving expenditure in excess of the upper range of the allocation to a school.

(ii) to pay special allowances to unqualified or temporary

teachers whom the authority thought to be insufficiently remunerated, in view of their experience or qualifications, by the prescribed scales.

(iii) to pay special allowances to head teachers whom the authority considered to be inadequately remunerated, in view of their duties and responsibilities.

(iv) to pay special allowances to mitigate or prevent hardship to teachers whose post ceased to exist, or whose salary was diminished, by the reorganization or closure of a school or department, or for any other good reason.

Payments from the pool were optional for authorities, and the only condition made about the amounts was that they should not effect a general alteration of the operation of the salary scales.

These additional allowances for 'special responsibility, special work of an advanced character, special academic, professional or industrial qualifications, or for other reasons which in the opinion of the Authority justify such allowances',[1] were payable to teachers in any type of school maintained by a local education authority. But the bulk of them always went to teachers in grammar schools and the 1951 scheme was undoubtedly designed to attract into these schools more men and women of high academic qualifications.

Throughout the years under review the grammar schools were gravely perturbed by the difficulty of obtaining such men and women, especially for the teaching of the natural sciences and mathematics. So serious was the shortage in these subjects that cases were known of schools going two or three years without being able to fill a vacancy. Some schools, conveniently close to one another, met the shortage by pooling their resources of staff, taking, say, physics at one school and biology at the other. Others simply had to reduce or even give up the teaching of one or more of the sciences.

[1] *Report of the Burnham Committee on Scales of Salaries in Primary and Secondary Schools*, 1951. H.M. Stationery Office, p. 8.

Such cases were exceptional. There was, indeed, throughout these years a tendency to exaggerate both the actual shortage of well qualified teachers in grammar schools and the number of teachers who left these schools for other kinds of employment. There were, it is true, more than normal opportunities during the immediate post-war years, especially in educational administration, industry, the civil service, and public corporations, for men and women with good academic qualifications; and the demand from industry for scientists and technologists persisted throughout. But such opportunities had always attracted such men and women away from teaching. The phenomenon was not new, nor was there anything approaching a wholesale 'flight from the grammar school', as its more ardent champions persisted in declaring.

Actually, the number of graduate teachers in grammar schools increased steadily at the rate of several hundreds a year; in 1947 there were 17,927, in 1951, 21,481. But the percentage decreased in the same period from 79 to 76.8: not a large drop, but sufficient to justify some apprehension. Against this drop must be set, however, a rise from 451 to 797 of teachers with qualifications recognized for salary purposes as equivalent to a university degree. If these teachers be regarded as graduates, the percentage drop was one and a half.

But there was a much more serious side to the matter. Though reliable figures are almost impossible to come by, there can be little doubt that the proportion of teachers with first-class honours degrees declined much more steeply than this, and that the proportion of third classes increased. That was, and still is, a cause for most serious concern. No one will deny that a third-class honours graduate may be every bit as good a teacher as a first-class, or a better one; but other things being equal he is not likely to be. Intelligence tells in teaching as in all other highly skilled occupations. And for advanced work in grammar schools first-rate academic qualifications are essential. The grammar school sixth forms contain the pick of the nation's intellectual ability, and they cannot be taught adequately by men and women who are only mediocre.

During these years the numbers of boys and girls in grammar school sixth forms increased prodigiously. In 1938 there were in the schools about 13,000 pupils aged 17 and upwards. By 1947 there were 25,000, and by 1951 close on 30,000. This increase threw an enormous strain upon the teaching resources of the grammar schools, a strain accentuated in many cases by lack of appropriate accommodation, apparatus and equipment for advanced work. Sixth form studies cannot be properly conducted in corridors or on the stages of assembly halls—as I saw being done—nor if first, second, and even third year sixth form pupils have to be taught together, as happened only too frequently owing to shortage of qualified staff.

The strain upon the grammar school staffs, already by that time severe, was not lightened by the drastic change in the external examination system which took place in 1951, when the General Certificate of Education replaced the School and Higher School Certificates which had held the field since 1917.

The Norwood Committee had in 1943 recommended the abolition of the School and Higher School Certificate examinations and the substitution in their place of a single examination at something below the level of the latter. Professional opinion was unstable; at first it tended to welcome the proposed change, but later hardened against it. The Minister therefore in 1946 referred the question to the Secondary School Examinations Council.

The Council reported[1] in August 1947. It recommended that:

(i) An examination at 'Ordinary', 'Advanced' and 'Scholarship' levels should be available each year to candidates who are at least 16 on 1st September. This minimum age should be raised, and the standard required at the 'Ordinary' level should be appropriately adjusted, when circumstances permit.

[1] *Examinations in Secondary Schools.* H.M. Stationery Office.

(ii) All subjects at all these levels should be purely optional.

(iii) A 'General Certificate of Education' should be awarded showing what subjects, and the level—'Ordinary' or 'Advanced'—in each subject, in which the candidate has satisfied the examiners.

The proposed changes meant very much more than the substitution of a single examination with papers at different levels for two separate and self-contained examinations. They implied a complete departure from the previously accepted purposes of external examinations for secondary schools—and consequently a complete reorganization of the curriculum for at least the upper part of the grammar school.

The School Certificate was designed to test the results of a course of general secondary education terminating at about the age of 16, and the Higher School Certificate to assess individual proficiency after a course, normally extending over two or three years, of specialized studies. To effect its designed purpose the School Certificate was made a grouped examination, that is, in order to pass a candidate had to attain the required standard in five subjects chosen from three main groups of subjects, and his proficiency in each group, not in each individual subject, was the criterion by which his success or failure was judged. Moreover, since the School Certificate was intended to measure, not only the candidate's but his school's proficiency, entire classes of pupils were normally entered.

From the start, however, the School Certificate was used by outside bodies for other purposes. The universities used it as a means of granting exemption from their entrance examination. The examining bodies of professional occupations similarly accepted a School Certificate pass (provided specified subjects were included) as exempting from their preliminary examinations. Thirdly, employers in general began to demand a School Certificate—and increasingly one of 'Matric.' standard —as a necessary qualification for clerical or other 'black-coated' occupations. Meanwhile the Higher School Certificate became increasingly used as a means for selecting recipients for State scholarships and local authority awards for university and other higher education.

It would not be correct to say that the School Certificate ever ceased to perform the function for which it was originally designed. Throughout the years it steadily improved academic standards in the schools; indeed, it was so successful in this that one of the main motives impelling change was a general feeling that the point had been reached at which such a yardstick was no longer necessary. On the other hand, employers, parents and the general public had come to regard it so universally as the necessary passport to non-manual employments, that this unintended function tended to dwarf all others. This had had profoundly harmful effects upon the work of the grammar schools, and the desire to eradicate these was among the main causes which prompted the change from the School Certificate to the General Certificate of Education.

The Secondary School Examinations Council decided that the time was ripe to do away with an examination—the School Certificate—whose educational purpose was merely to assess the results of a four or five years' course of general secondary education. It set itself to devise an examination to serve the needs of those pupils who aimed to go on to higher studies or who desired on leaving school 'a national credential for a definite purpose'.[1] It had particularly in mind:

(*a*) Those who wish to compete for scholarships or similar awards at universities or comparable establishments of further education.

(*b*) Those who have followed courses substantially beyond the statutory minimum leaving-age and who wish to secure exemption from university or professional examinations.[2]

[1] *Examinations in Secondary Schools.* Ministry of Education Circular 256, dated 4th September 1952.
[2] *Report of the Secondary School Examinations Council 1947.*

The essential difference, then, between the General Certificate of Education and the School Certificate was that whereas the latter looked back, and assessed the value of what had been done, the former looked forward and attempted to assess the candidate's capacity to go on to more advanced studies. The General Certificate, as the Ministry of Education emphasized in Circular 256, 'served to testify to a degree of mastery in the particular subjects which should be secure and usable for the future'. That being its function, it was essential that, as the Secondary School Examinations Council pointed out in their 1948 Report,[1] it should be taken 'as late as possible in the school career, and therefore as close as possible to the change to further education or entry into a career with which [it is] associated'.

A large number of grammar school teachers failed at first to grasp this fundamental point of difference between the old and the new examinations. Had they appreciated it they would not, I think, have opposed so strenuously or so unanimously the imposition of a minimum age of entry for the General Certificate of Education—though admittedly it was a tactless error to make the limit so inflexible: the compromise later arrived at was so eminently sensible that one wonders why it was not thought of at the beginning.

The opposition to the fixed minimum age of 16 for entry never abated until the terms of the regulation were relaxed in 1952. It was based largely on the argument that if the General Certificate of Education could not be taken before the age of 16 there would be insufficient time available for the specialized studies of the sixth form. In fact, a check to too early intensive specialization was one of the objectives the Ministry had in mind. But this was only one item—albeit a most important one—in a larger purpose: to restore the grammar school curriculum to its medieval and, as many people believe, still its proper function, that of laying the foundation for advanced

[1] p. 5.

academic studies. This seems clear from the following passage in *The New Secondary Education*.

'... the grammar school course is coming to be regarded as a single whole from 11 to 18, the earlier part of which should lead naturally on to the later part and *should no longer be conceived as a course complete in itself to which a few pupils add an extra period of one or two years* ...

'With a six or seven years' course so conceived, and *with any external examinations that may be taken placed at the point at which their purposes are seen to be relevant*, many of the difficulties that now beset the curriculum would be removed.' (*Italics mine.*)

All teachers, whether engaged in university or school teaching, were agreed in principle that the prolonged period of narrow specialization which was becoming all too common in grammar school sixth forms, especially on the science side, was definitely harmful. In principle, everyone wished to diminish the undoubted strain this put upon pupils and the narrowing effect it had upon their minds. It was therefore all to the good that the universities decided to insist upon success in a broad course of studies as a qualification for university entry. After prolonged deliberations the Committee of Vice-Chancellors and Principals announced in January 1949 that any candidate wishing to gain exemption from a university entrance examination by way of the G.C.E. had to fulfil the following conditions:

(i) Obtain a pass in English Language and in either four or five other subjects.

(ii) These subjects must include (*a*) a language other than English, and (*b*) either mathematics or an approved science.

(iii) At least two of the subjects must be passed at the Advanced level.

(iv) Candidates who offered only four subjects in addition to English Language must pass at one and the same sitting in two subjects at the Advanced level and in one other subject not related to the subjects at the Advanced level.

The teacher training colleges and the professional associations followed this lead. The training colleges required as minimum academic qualifications for entry:

'Passes in five subjects at Ordinary level, or four subjects at Ordinary and one at Advanced, or two subjects at Ordinary and two at Advanced, or three subjects at Advanced, and evidence of having studied other subjects to a reasonable standard.'

The requirements of the professional bodies varied in accordance with the nature of the occupations they represented. For example, the Law Society demanded,[1] for exemption from their preliminary examination:

'Either

(a) passes at Ordinary level in the course of not more than two examinations in five subjects, of which three must be (i) English language, English, or English literature, (ii) Latin, and (iii) history, and the other two may include one of the English subjects not offered under (i).

Or

(b) passes (not necessarily in the course of one or two examinations) in three subjects, at least two being at Advanced level, and one subject at Ordinary level, of which two must be (i) English language, English, or English literature, and (ii) Latin.'

The Chartered Institute of Secretaries required four passes at Ordinary level, including (i) English, (ii) mathematics, (iii) history or geography, and (iv) Latin, a modern language, a natural science, or the subject not taken under (iii). The various engineering institutions and the Royal Aeronautical Society also demanded four Ordinary passes, but these had to include in addition to English (i) mathematics, and (ii) either two approved science subjects or one approved science subject and a language other than English.

It will be seen that these various requirements all upheld the principle of a broad general education, though in the case

[1] See Circular 227 (revised), dated 16th September 1952.

of the professional bodies this was naturally to some extent biased in favour of the occupations they represented. The requirements meant, in fact, that candidates for higher education or professional employment had to pass an examination which in breadth was similar to the School Certificate, but pitched at a somewhat higher level. But, thanks to the fact that the G.C.E. examination was placed on a subject, not a group, basis the process of securing such qualifications was, despite the higher standard demanded, rendered at once less exacting and hazardous than before. It could be spread over a period of years, and so taken in one's stride; and the depressing experience of having to take the entire examination again if one failed at the first attempt was eliminated.

Needless to say, the more enterprising among the grammar schools quickly found ways of adapting their organization to meet the new situation. While these varied in detail, they were in general based on the arrangement of separate courses for pupils intending to go on to higher education and those expecting to leave school shortly after taking the examination for the General Certificate. Then, in April 1952, the regulation enforcing a minimum age for entry was relaxed.

The late Mr. George Tomlinson while he was Minister of Education persistently refused to rescind this regulation. When, in October 1951, a Conservative government was returned to power his successor, Miss Florence Horsbrugh, remitted this and other matters to the Secondary School Examinations Council. Early in the New Year they presented to her a brief report,[1] in which they recommended that the age limit should be retained but that the head of a school should have full discretion to enter a pupil for the examination at a lower age if he were prepared to certify that:

(a) It was educationally desirable that the pupil should take the examination in the particular subjects offered at the time proposed;

[1] *Examinations in Secondary Schools.* H.M. Stationery Office, 1952.

(*b*) The pupil had pursued a course of study with such a degree of competence as to make it very probable that he would pass in the subjects offered.

On 24th April 1952, Miss Horsbrugh announced in the House of Commons that she had accepted this and the other recommendations made by the S.S.E.C. At the time of writing it is too early to say what use will be made of this measure of freedom. It seems to lay a heavy responsibility upon heads of schools. No definition of 'educationally desirable' was given in the S.S.E.C. report, nor was there any hint as to whether 'certify' meant merely offering an opinion or actually putting one's signature to a formal declaration. It does, however, mean that the able child may go ahead at his own proper pace.

To put an end to the still widespread misunderstanding about the G.C.E. the Ministry of Education issued Circular 256 (4th September 1952), which included the following passage:

'The General Certificate of Education sets out to give the maximum freedom from examinations . . . [it] is a new examination with a more limited purpose than its predecessors. It looks forward rather than back and serves to testify to a degree of mastery in the particular subjects which should be secure and usable for the future. It is designed with a full secondary course in mind and has particular relevance to university and professional qualifications, though it is also adapted to school leavers of 16+ who want national qualifications of suitable standard.

'It is intended that only those who have a reasonable chance of getting a pass should be entered at all for any particular subject . . . It is . . . not an examination designed for school leavers as such . . . '

There could be no misunderstanding those words. Two other points made in the circular were that the Ordinary and Advanced papers were not to be regarded as constituting successive examinations and that the former practice of entering whole classes for examination was to be abandoned.

There can be little doubt that the introduction of this examination will exercise considerable influence on the organization, the methods and the work of the grammar school. How much, and in what directions, it is difficult to estimate. But at the time of writing it seems hardly likely to be one of the main factors determining the future of the grammar school. These, I think, are three in number.

First, the increase or decrease in pressure from parents to get their children into grammar schools rather than into schools of any other type. That in turn depends largely upon, first, the development of the modern school, and secondly the extent to which bilateral and other amalgamations take place. I do not think that the comprehensive or the multilateral school seriously threatens the grammar school as a separate entity, but I do think that widespread bilateralism might turn the grammar school into a much more selective institution.

Secondly, the increase or decrease in the proportion of early withdrawals from grammar schools: and by early withdrawals I mean withdrawals before the age of 17 or 18, and not merely those which take place at the end of compulsory school age. A continued high proportion of these might well tend to a large increase of bilateral schools, or even the comprehensive schools up to the age of 15 proposed in 1953 by the Labour Party, for those pupils unlikely to remain at school to 17 or 18. This proposal would have the effect of turning the grammar school proper into a highly selective school, having as its principal, if not sole, function preparation for entry to the university.

Thirdly, at the other end of the scale, the increase or decrease in the proportion of grammar school pupils remaining at school until the age of 18+. This very largely depends upon university policy about numbers. A decision to stabilize or reduce the number of university students would inevitably check the growth in the numbers of pupils in sixth forms: and the size of the sixth form relative to the whole school has a crucial bearing upon the character of the grammar school.

These three factors all pose the question: will the grammar school tend to become a small, extremely selective institution with very high academic standards, or the school for all children with recognizably academic leanings? Each of these developments had its advocates during the years here under review, and the question at times became a matter for controversy. By 1952 I had put the chances of either happening at about fifty-fifty, but at the moment of writing, twelve months later, I am inclined to think the more selective institution a safer bet—provided always that the necessary annual recruitment of highly qualified graduate teachers can be secured. It would be foolish in the extreme to hazard any opinion about the possibility of that beyond, perhaps, speculating that the years of the abnormally large birth rate might by 1965 or so be beginning to produce the required strength.

Other evidence that might indicate the future development of the grammar school is confusing. Up till 1951 the number of pupils remaining at grammar schools beyond the age of compulsion rose steadily and swiftly; in 1938 it was 138,000, in 1951, 203,000. In the latter year, however, there were suggestions that the numbers were falling, though only slightly. At the same time there was an increase in the number of early withdrawals (i.e., before the age of 16), which were then running at about 25 per cent. This was not, as many people imagined, an unprecedentedly high rate; up to 1938, in fact, the percentage was in most years appreciably higher. But it was sufficiently large to threaten the whole conception of a school providing a seven-years' course from 11 to 18.

These early withdrawals were, many of them, made, either genuinely or ostensibly, for economic reasons. They were markedly more numerous in districts where the demand for juvenile labour was pressing, and undoubtedly many people were feeling severely the pinch of rising prices. But they were also evidence that the grammar school had not yet succeeded in finding its precise function in the new educational system.

Though undoubtedly some—perhaps many—children who could have profited by remaining at school, and some even who would have qualified for entry to university, were withdrawn because of the poverty, cupidity, or ignorance of their parents, on the whole those who left early were pupils who were not standing up too well to the academic disciplines of the grammar school. While it would be too severe a judgement to call them failures, they were certainly not successes.

In other words, the academic standards of the grammar school were too high for them. Yet the setting of a higher pass standard for the G.C.E. than for the School Certificate meant that the general standard of the schools' work would have to be raised. Up to 1952 neither the Ministry, the local education authorities, nor the teachers had given evidence that they were getting to grips with the implications of this; that, in brief, they were making a serious attempt to discover approximately what proportion of the school population was intellectually sufficiently able to undertake grammar school studies. Upon the resolution of this question depends in the final analysis the future of the grammar school, and, more important, the quality of the education the nation's ablest children will receive.

TECHNICAL SECONDARY EDUCATION

The distinguishing feature of the secondary technical school, wrote the Ministry of Education in *The New Secondary Education*,[1] 'is its relationship to a particular industry or occupation or group of industries and occupations'. In April 1945, when it graduated to secondary rank, the technical school had several other features which distinguished it from grammar or modern schools.

First, it was not a homogeneous unit but a group of schools: junior technical, junior commercial, and junior art departments. Second, these had different ages of entry and exit, and

[1] p. 47.

different lengths of course. Most of the junior technical schools for boys recruited their pupils at about 12½ to 13, and gave them a three-year course; most of the few junior technical schools for girls (domestic subjects and women's crafts), though recruiting at approximately the same age, gave a two-year course only. So did most of the junior commercial schools and the junior art departments, and the latter recruited at every age from 11 to 14. The only point in which they all agreed in these respects was in being different from either the grammar or the modern school. Third, few of them had their own premises; most of the junior technical and junior commercial schools were housed in technical colleges, and all the junior art departments, as their name implied, were attached to adult art schools or colleges. Fourth, some at least, especially among the junior art departments, were much nearer to being trade training schools than schools of general education. Fifth —and this was more important than might seem—they were very few in numbers, and with the rarest exceptions confined to large towns.

All these reasons made it difficult for them to be easily assimilated into the new secondary system. Nor in most cases were the difficulties removed by 1952; the majority retained their later age of entry and remained housed in adult institutions. Because of their later entry age, and because they were, as always previously, highly successful in placing their leavers in skilled employment, they were regarded in many places (as they had been when junior technical schools) as a way of escape from the modern school for pupils who had no chance of reaching the grammar school. On the other hand, despite the Ministry's assertion, in *The New Secondary Education*,[1] that 'To assume that the "top layer" in intelligence will always go to the grammar school would be contrary to the purpose of the 1944 Act', few really able children offered grammar school places turned them down in favour of the secondary technical school.

[1] p. 54.

Again, though the Ministry had insisted[1] that 'provision at the sixth form level must be available for those boys and girls who want it and can profit by it', the very success of the secondary technical school in placing its pupils in apprenticeships (which had to be taken up between the ages of $15\frac{1}{2}$ and $16\frac{1}{2}$) usually precluded the possibility of a sixth form.

There were exceptions to all these generalizations; the Gateway School at Leicester, for example, with which I was once connected, had its own fine premises and a strong sixth form. But the Gateway had been an exceptional school from its birth, and it would probably be found that most of the other secondary technical schools which transcended the normal limitations had a somewhat unusual history behind them. Either that, or, as in one case I know, they had come under the care of an exceptionally able and imaginative head. The majority remained rather uneasily poised in a somewhat peculiar intermediate position between the grammar and the modern schools.

In the circumstances it was not surprising that many educational administrators began to wonder whether there was really any place for the secondary technical school in the new system. The grammar school, they thought, could undertake its more advanced and more academic work, and the modern school the more elementary and practical work up to the age of 15 or 16. The secondary technical school had its devoted supporters, but they were either reluctant to make their voices heard or singularly unsuccessful in doing so; far less was said in public or written for publication about the secondary technical school than about either of the other two types. Even the Ministry, usually so fair in its distribution of favours, in its six-page survey of the quality of education in primary and secondary schools published in its Report of 1949,[2] could find room for only three depressing sentences about it.

'The secondary technical schools as a whole have hardly yet

[1] *ibid.*, p. 57.   [2] p. 24.

had time or opportunity to outgrow the limitations imposed by their history. Too often they fail to obtain a fair share of the abler pupils because their age of entry is higher than that to the grammar schools. This in turn is often due to the fact that the school is housed in a technical college whose accommodation, already under pressure, cannot by any means be stretched to make possible the organization of a course lasting from 11 to 16 or 18.'

The passage, it will be seen, contains not one word about the quality of the work being done in secondary technical schools. That was a pity, for the work in some of them was absolutely first-rate. Admittedly, in some cases it was almost undiluted vocational training, but in others, as I saw from personal visits, boys and girls were being given as broad and liberal education as could be found in any secondary schools in the country.

The number of maintained secondary technical schools decreased between 1947 and 1952 from 317 to 291, though the number of pupils in such schools increased by about 10 per cent, from 66,454 to 74,329. There were in 1952 indications that the number of schools would decline still further; principally by amalgamation in bilateral schools, of which there were in 1952 already twenty-three with a technical side. Prophecy is always dangerous, but I will venture the opinion that the secondary technical school will maintain its independent existence only in districts (including rural districts) where one or more groups of related skilled occupations predominate, but that there it will be strong, successful, and highly esteemed.

Chapter Four

OPPORTUNITIES FOR ADULTS

VOCATIONAL TRAINING

SOMETHING of the war-time effort of the technical colleges was told in my previous volume.[1] In June 1946 the Ministry of Education, in A.M. 165 (17th June 1946), published figures showing that during the war 288,992 persons (241,334 men and 47,658 women) received special courses of training in technical colleges and other establishments of further education. 'The work', added the Ministry, 'was done under adverse conditions, and the excellent results obtained would have been impossible without the eager co-operation and unflagging effort of local education authorities, governing bodies, principals and staffs.'

The work of the colleges continued after the war without a break, with no slackening of intensity, and under almost equally adverse conditions. As early as May 1945 the Ministry, in Circular 48 (24th May 1945), was drawing the attention of local education authorities to urgent tasks in which the help of the colleges was required. Foremost among these was the provision of a wide variety of full-time training courses, under the resettlement scheme of the Ministry of Labour, to fit demobilized men and women to enter, or re-enter, civilian employment. A second task was to train large numbers of men and boys for the building trades in order that the ravages of war might be made good.

These two large-scale undertakings would by themselves have put sufficient strain upon the resources of the colleges. But

[1] *Education in Transition*, pp. 131–6.

public as well as official demand began also to press upon them. If the Ministries of Labour and Education had their ideas about priorities, so had the man in the street—and the two by no means always coincided. Moreover, there had been in progress since 1943 a renascence of apprenticeship, and employers were clamouring for courses for their apprentices and learners.

As during the war, the colleges met the challenge with a magnificent response. Their most difficult problem was to find accommodation for the vast host of would-be students that was queueing at their doors. With men and women pouring out of the forces and war industries they had, at first at any rate, little difficulty in recruiting additional staff; but where to house their ever-growing student population was a problem which soon assumed a nightmare complexion. It was all very well for the Ministry to tell them, as it did in Circular 57 (9th July 1945), to expand their premises. But how? New building was impossible, and adaptation of existing structures almost as difficult to get done. The local authorities bought, leased or rented whatever properties they could lay their hands on. Industry helped by offering accommodation where it could. But demand always far outstripped supply. A passage in the Ministry of Education's Report for 1948,[1] in which a survey of progress was made, gives some idea of the straits in which many colleges still found themselves:

'Classes overflowed into huts, schools, factories and warehouses; laboratories were on occasion used as classrooms, and classrooms as laboratories . . . classes started early and continued late; stores were shifted out into corridors so that storerooms could be used for teaching; rooms were overcrowded. By 1948 it was rare indeed to find a college or school where accommodation was adequate . . .'

[1] *Education in 1948.* H.M. Stationery Office, 1949, pp. 41-2. The same statements could be made in 1952, as witness the Report of the Select Committee on Estimates on Technical Education, published in August 1953.

Far from being exaggerated, the passage may be considered to err on the side of understatement. Late in 1947 I myself saw classes being held in corridors, staff-rooms and refectories; in condemned dwelling-houses, disused schools and derelict chapels; and in one case in a former mortuary. I saw architectural students so closely packed at their drawing boards that their elbows touched, and machine tools huddled so thickly in workshops that it was difficult to pick one's way between them. Even so the colleges often had insufficient equipment; one of the most serious consequences of universal overcrowding was that it greatly diminished the time for the practical work which is so essential in vocational courses.

This huge and varied pressure upon the technical colleges was evidence of the fact that, as the Ministry's 1948 Report noted, 'Further education in this country is passing through a revolution'. That revolution, which is still in full spate, has two main facets. First, to quote the 1948 Report again:[1]

'... partly as a result of war experience, partly because our economic situation was so obviously dangerous, the ideas of employers, educationists and the general public had advanced far beyond those of 1939. Students came forward for training in greater numbers than ever before, and, owing to technological advances in industry, required a greater variety of courses.'

Secondly—and this is the really revolutionary feature—the whole structure of the vocational side of further education was rapidly altering.

'... the tradition of part-time evening instruction, which had grown up in response to local and often haphazard demands, was giving place to a planned system with an emphasis on training during the daytime.'[2]

This did not mean, it should at once be added, that the number of evening students was decreasing. On the contrary, it increased progressively and sharply after the war. In 1946-7, at 1,350,000 it was already substantially above the 1937-8

[1] p. 41. [2] p. 38.

figure of 1,178,863. The following year it rose to 1,540,000, and by 1951 it had passed the 2 million mark. What it did mean was that technical colleges which before the war had been almost empty during the day, or at best half full, were now crowded to overflowing from early morning until late at night.

It is true that, as the 1948 Report noted, this change was already under way before the war. But it was then making only slow and fitful progress. After the war, though hampered at every turn by persisting shortages of accommodation, equipment and, later, staff, it strode ahead rapidly and surely. The phenomenal increase in the number of young employees released by their firms for part-time education and training during working hours was its most spectacular illustration, though it must be emphasized that this was only one aspect of a change affecting all types of vocational training.

In 1938 some 40,000 young employees, mainly engaged in engineering trades, were being given systematic education and training during working hours. In the early years of the war this figure dropped to about 31,000. But in 1943 the Ministry of Labour and National Service sent a round robin to industry asking it to examine the whole problem of the recruitment and training of young people after the war. In particular, industry was requested to consider the principle of national apprenticeship schemes in all skilled occupations, to include as an essential feature regular part-time education and training within working hours.

By 1945 some fifty sections of industry had drawn up and signed such schemes, and the number of young people under daytime instruction had risen significantly. Thereafter this went up by leaps and bounds. By 1947 it had grown to over 167,000—four times the figure of 1938—by 1948 to 190,000, and by 1952, when the number of participating occupations had risen to over eighty, to almost 300,000. Striking as was this expansion, there is no doubt that had the technical colleges, and industry, been able to provide more accommodation, equipment and staff it would have been far larger. On various visits which I made between 1947 and 1952 I was told in town after town the same story of demand which could not be met, even to 'whole trades queueing up', as one education officer put it.

As before the war, the engineering trades contributed far more students than any other group of occupations, but—a significantly encouraging pointer to the growing breadth of the movement—in a rapidly diminishing proportion. In 1946–7 engineering students made up more than half the total number, in 1947–8 they were fewer than half, and by 1951–2 only just over one-third. By 1947–8 the building and mining industries were sending substantial numbers, and all Government Departments and some local authorities were releasing their young employees. By 1951–2 agriculture, commercial and professional occupations and personal and domestic services were also contributing relatively large numbers.

Nearly one-quarter of all young employees being released in 1951–2 were taking courses of general education. Some of these were young people engaged in unskilled or only slightly skilled occupations which required no prolonged period of practical training or any considerable amount of theoretical knowledge; but the great majority of them—more than five out of every seven—were preparing for various professional preliminary examinations. The driving force behind this part-time day release movement was without question the desire to improve vocational efficiency.

As the bulk of students came from skilled trades, it was only to be expected that the number of passes in the examinations related to these trades would rise rapidly. Such was the case, though unfortunately the number of failures increased also— evidence that many young people were attempting courses beyond them. There was, too, a growing number of apprentices and others who did not even get so far as the first public examination for their trade, but dropped out in the first or second year of the course. The number of Ordinary and Higher National Certificates—the technician's qualifications—leaped upwards. In 1944 they only just exceeded the figure of 1939 (4,070 as against 3,999). By 1948 the number of Ordinary Certificates had more than trebled and that of Higher doubled; in 1952 nearly six times as many Higher National Certificates were gained as in 1938—conclusive evidence that standards as well as numbers were rising. The range of demand increased; to meet this several new certificates were created: for applied chemistry, applied physics, metallurgy, production engineering, mining, and retail distribution. There were similar increases in the numbers obtaining the craftsmen's certificates offered by the City and Guilds of London Institute and the various regional bodies such as the Union of Lancashire and Cheshire Institutes. In 1951 the City and Guilds awarded some 50,000 certificates and—another indication that the reserves of quality were growing—instituted an Insignia award ranking above all their other certificates.

An important feature of the day release movement was its widespread extension to employees beyond the age of apprenticeship. In 1948 one-sixth of all students released were over the age of 20. The proportion declined later with the rapid growth in the number of apprentices and learners released, but in 1952 it was still one in eight. This is not including the considerable number of employees released for full-time courses, including university courses.

Many industries and firms had regular arrangements for sending employees to such full-time courses. The largest scheme was that of the National Coal Board, which from 1947 onwards offered annually up to a hundred university scholarships; fifty to boys on leaving school and fifty to men already in the industry. These scholarships, which were for the study of mining engineering and allied subjects, covered all tuition and examination fees, and carried in addition maintenance grants of up to £300 a year. It is sad to have to record that in none of the five years between 1947 and 1952 did sufficient schoolboys of good enough quality offer themselves to enable the full number of scholarships to be awarded. But there was no difficulty in finding suitable candidates within the industry.

The rapidly growing demand from industry for advanced courses in technological subjects led to a number of important developments in the organization of technical education; and, unfortunately, to an unhappy controversy which wound its wearisome way throughout the whole period under review and was still unresolved in 1952.

It had been evident to many people before the war that the populations of many local education authorities were too small to support a technical college providing a wide range of advanced studies. This was a main theme of the Report on Higher Technological Education[1] made in 1944 by a Departmental Committee under the chairmanship of Lord Eustace Percy, a former President of the Board of Education, and then Vice-Chancellor of Durham University.

The 'Percy' Report recommended the establishment throughout the country of Regional Advisory Councils for Further Education, with, it proposed, Regional Academic Boards, representative of the teaching staffs of universities and technical colleges, to advise upon the provision of advanced courses in technological subjects.

In Circular 87 (20th February 1946) the Minister announced that she had accepted these recommendations and invited the local education authorities to get together and discuss with the universities and university colleges in their areas the setting up, in regions where they did not already exist,[2] of appro-

[1] H.M. Stationery Office, 1944.
[2] Five regional councils for further education already existed: The Yorkshire Council for Further Education, The Advisory Council for Technical Education for South Wales and Monmouthshire, The West Midlands Advisory Council, The Regional Advisory Council for Technical and Other Forms of Further Education for Manchester and District, and The Merseyside Regional Advisory Council for Further Education.

priately constituted regional bodies. The circular suggested the following ten regions:

1. Metropolitan and Home Counties.
2. Southern.
3. Western.
4. West Midlands.
5. East Midlands.
6. East Anglia.
7. Yorkshire.
8. North Western.
9. Northern.
10. Wales and Monmouthshire.

By the end of 1947 the proposed Councils and Academic Boards had been set up in all these regions. In 1948, as a natural corollary, the Minister established a National Advisory Council on Education for Industry and Commerce, to co-ordinate the work of the Regional Councils and advise on matters of national policy. This somewhat cumbrous body comprised seventy-two members, of whom fifty-two were nominated by the Regional Advisory Councils and twenty by the Minister of Education. The first chairman was Lieutenant-General Sir Ronald M. Weeks, formerly Deputy Chief of the Imperial General Staff, and at the time Deputy Chairman of Vickers, Ltd.

The duties of the National Council were officially declared[1] to include:

'... advice to the Minister on the whole range of national policy necessary for the development of education in relation to industry and commerce, including training for management and design and the allied professions, the maintenance of contact at the national level with industry and commerce and appropriate professional bodies, and the task of negotiation with the

---
[1] *Education in 1948*, p. 39.

University Grants Committee and other appropriate bodies on all matters relating to education in advanced technology.'

Among the matters to which the Council immediately addressed itself, in co-operation with the University Grants Committee (which established for the purpose a technological subcommittee), were the following:[1]

(a) the training and education of technologists and applied scientists of the highest type required by industry;

(b) the education of the technologist at other levels with a view to the creation of an orderly national scheme in which both universities and technical colleges should play their part without overlapping or waste of effort;

(c) the future training of mechanical and electrical engineers in Government service;

(d) over-specialization as it affected the training of technologists;

(e) qualifications of technical State scholars for admission to universities.

It cannot be said that entirely satisfactory answers were found to any of these questions during the period under review. That was perhaps hardly to be expected; but unhappily counsels were darkened by the persistent fog of controversy which enfolded items (a) and (b).

The very difficult question of the relationship between the universities and the technical colleges had been fruitlessly debated for some years before the National Council was created. The principal issue at stake was not so much the respective parts which universities and technical colleges should play in providing higher technological education (though that was much discussed) as the relative value of the awards to be obtained on completion of university and technical college courses. To put the matter bluntly, the technical colleges were out for 'parity of esteem', the universities against it.

A strong body of opinion in the colleges desired for them the

[1] *ibid.*, pp. 39–40.

right to grant degrees. To this the universities were inflexibly opposed. Other proposals from the technical side were that colleges should be affiliated to universities (after the London pattern), that they should be upgraded to university college status, or that one or more universities of technology should be created. After discussions which went on for years a façade of agreement (it was no more) was secured, and the National Advisory Council for Education in Industry and Commerce accordingly recommended[1] to the Minister late in 1950 the establishment of a Royal College of Technologists. This body, it was proposed, would admit Members by examination and confer the status of Fellow in respect of distinguished work or services. Departments of technical colleges which satisfied the requirements of the Royal College could obtain the right to prepare students for the Membership examination. This right, it was argued, would set the hallmark of excellence upon the work of these departments.

Everyone expected that this scheme, to which all the professional bodies concerned had more or less willingly subscribed, would be almost automatically accepted by the Government. Actually, the Labour Government did accept it; one of its last acts before going out of office in November 1951 was to issue a White Paper[2] which in general accepted the recommendations of the National Advisory Council. But the Conservative Government which succeeded had other views. In June 1952 Miss Florence Horsbrugh, the Minister of Education, announced that the idea of a Royal College of Technologists had been abandoned. Instead, the Government had decided to establish in the near future a university of technology. This was the one solution which almost all parties to the long controversy had agreed was immediately the least practicable.

The next month the Ministry of Education, in Circular 255

[1] *Report on the Future Development of Higher Technological Education.* H.M. Stationery Office, 1950.
[2] *Higher Technological Education.* Cmd. 8357. H.M. Stationery Office, 1951.

(14th July 1952), offered grant at the rate of 75 per cent instead of the normal 60 per cent for approved courses in advanced technology at technical colleges. To qualify, stated the circular, courses would have to fit industrial needs and the national pattern for technological education, and colleges would have to show that their staffing, space and equipment were adequate. How substantial an 'upgrading' this will mean the future must be left to show.

It must not be assumed from the continuance of this long drawn-out controversy that there were no developments in higher technological education during these years. On the contrary, the period was fruitful of them. What will probably prove in the long run to be the most important is the one least susceptible to detailed documentation: the progressive concentration of the more advanced studies in major technical colleges and the complementary transfer of more elementary work to branch establishments. Another important development difficult to document precisely was the increase of research in the technical colleges.

Strong encouragement to the colleges to engage in research was given by the Ministry in Circular 94 (8th April 1946). 'The main function of Technical Colleges', said the circular, 'is the advancement and dissemination of knowledge, especially knowledge of value to industry . . .'

'Here the importance and educational value of research work cannot be over-emphasized . . . To-day it is more than ever important, if we are to restore and enhance our industrial position and attain full employment and an improved standard of life, to ensure that scientific and technical research is carried out as widely and intensively as possible and applied promptly to production. To such research the Technical Colleges should make their contribution . . .'

'The time has come', added the circular, 'to recognize that research should be regarded as a normal and, indeed, an important function of the Technical Colleges.' 'Probably the most important and suitable type of research', it was suggested, 'is applied research undertaken at the direct or indirect suggestion of industry'—though fundamental research was not to be excluded. But it must be genuine research; 'routine testing on behalf of local industry . . . should only be done when industrial facilities are not available'.

Research should not, warned the circular, be pursued to the extent of interfering with the proper discharge of teaching duties. As a rough guide, the Ministry suggested that up to two-fifths of a full-time teacher's time might be taken up with research, though 'considerable latitude' should be allowed in the case of applied research of pressing importance. Moreover, 'it is very desirable that teachers should carry out research with their senior students, thus giving these experience in research work' and 'the research approach to scientific and industrial problems'. Such research could be carried out in teaching time.

It is impossible to give any idea how much research was done in technical colleges, but that its volume was considerable and the quality of much of it high is evident from the fact that between 1945 and 1951, 196 papers of original research were published by people working in technical colleges.

More probably would have been done but for another important development. In Circular 98 (10th April 1946), published, as will be noted, almost simultaneously with Circular 94, the Ministry invited the co-operation of technical colleges possessing appropriate accommodation in 'the establishment within them of national schools or departments, directed to particular branches of technology'. Each of these schools, it was hoped, would 'be recognized by the industry concerned as the national centre to which it looks to provide advanced technological education and appropriate research work'. Though to be housed for the time being in a technical college, each national school was to be regarded as a separate entity, and administered by an autonomous governing body, which would include national representatives of the industry concerned.

Grant to cover the entire net cost of the school would be paid direct to the governing body by the Minister.

The first such 'school' to be established was the National College of Horology and Instrument Technology. (They have all been called 'Colleges', despite the Ministry's description of them as 'schools'.) This was opened on 6th October 1947, in the Northampton Polytechnic, which is situated in the district of Clerkenwell in London—long famed as a centre of watch and clock making. It was followed by colleges of rubber technology (Northern Polytechnic, London, 1948), heating, ventilating, refrigeration and fan engineering (Borough Polytechnic, London, 1948), foundry (Wolverhampton Technical College, 1948), leather technology (Leathersellers' College, Smithfield, London, 1951), and food technology (Cranwood Street, London, 1952).

All these colleges were in 1952 still small, none having more than a hundred students. Some offered two, some three types of course. At the College of Horology, for example, there were three courses: a general full-time course for students aged 16 and upwards who wished to qualify as technicians; a longer part-time course on a 'sandwich' basis leading to the same qualification; and a full-time advanced course of two years designed to train potential executives. At the College of Food Technology there were two post-graduate courses, in applied microbiology and canning, each of six months' duration, and a two-year full-time course in general food technology. The conduct of research, both fundamental and applied, is a function of all the colleges; and this has necessarily drawn away some research from the technical colleges proper. The department of rubber technology at the Northern Polytechnic, for example, which became the National College, was already widely famous for its brilliant research.

On a somewhat different basis but having the same aim of providing specialized technological education at the highest level, is the College of Aeronautics, opened at Cranfield, Bedfordshire, on 15th October 1946. Sited on a R.A.F. Station, this college is not only much larger than the others and possessed of its own premises (as some others are in process of becoming), but designed for work of post-graduate quality only (though the possession of a degree has never been an obligatory condition of entry, and in fact many good students have entered either on a Higher National Certificate or from the officer ranks of the Royal Navy or the R.A.F.). From the start, too, entry was thrown open to all the countries in the British Commonwealth.

Unlike the other national colleges, Cranfield is almost entirely residential, and its administration more nearly approaches that of a university than theirs. Though it is entirely financed by the Ministry of Education and its policy is controlled by a Board of Governors appointed by the Minister, its academic organization is directed by a senate consisting of the Principal and the heads of teaching departments.

The course lasts two years. In the first year, which is the same for all students, a broad knowledge of aeronautics is assured. In the second, students branch off into various specialist fields. During this year every student 'is required to prepare a thesis on a subject chosen in consultation with the academic staff, and to carry out some experimental research or undertake a piece of design work in addition, though this may well be related to his thesis work'.[1] Successful students are awarded the Diploma of the College (D.C.Ae.), and outstanding merit is recognized by the endorsement 'with Distinction'.

In a different category again is the reorganized Royal College of Art. Founded in 1837 as the 'School of Design' and intended to give a practical training to artisans and designers, the college had tended throughout its history to be diverted from its original purpose by the attraction for its students (and teachers) of the fine arts. In 1935 a committee appointed, under the chairmanship of Viscount Hambleden, to re-examine its functions, recommended its re-equipment as a national school of design. Directly after the war this reorganization was

[1] Extract from the college prospectus.

begun. The college was rehoused in greatly enlarged premises, completely re-equipped, and organized in ten schools grouped into four faculties.[1] Each school is in the charge of a professor. In addition to the diploma previously awarded by the college, the A.R.C.A., a new one, 'Designer R.C.A.', was created for students in the Industrial Design Faculties. It was made a condition of this award that students should, after finishing the course, spend not less than nine months in approved employment in industry. On 1st April 1949 the college was established as a National College, financed and administered exactly like the others.

No account of the development of vocational education since the war would be adequate without reference to the amazing growth, from about 1948 onwards, of what was generically called 'education for management'. Before the war this term was rarely heard, but after the report of the 'Urwick' Committee,[2] appointed by the Minister of Education, on *Education for Management*, published in 1947, instruction in managerial and supervisory duties spread like wildfire. In 1947 the British Institute of Management, a Government-sponsored body, was formed to stimulate and aid the movement. The British Association of Commercial and Industrial Education (BACIE) and its affiliated organizations took it up vigorously, and by 1952 there were every week scores of courses and conferences discussing this, that, or the other aspect of the subject.

The movement covered all ranks in industry, but concentrated especially upon instructing foremen and supervisors, and devoted particular attention to teaching them how to

---

[1] *Faculty of Fine Arts*—Schools of Engraving, Painting, Sculpture, and Architecture.

Faculty of Industrial Arts—Schools of Engineering and Furniture Design, Silversmithing and Jewellery, Textiles, Ceramics, and Architecture.

Faculty of Fashion—Schools of Fashion Design, Textiles, Silversmithing and Jewellery.

Faculty of Graphic Design—Schools of Graphic Design, Painting and Engraving.

[2] The chairman was Lt.-Col. L. Urwick.

improve the human relationships in shop and factory. The interest these functionaries showed in their own betterment was demonstrated by the rapid growth of the Institute of Industrial Supervisors which, founded in November 1948, had within a couple of years nineteen self-governing branches spread over the country from London to Glasgow.

While attention was largely focused on the lower ranks of management, the upper were not neglected. The most notable effort on behalf of these was the establishment in 1948, by a group of people drawn from private enterprise and the public services, of the Administrative Staff College. Housed in an attractive building near Henley-on-Thames, this college set out to:[1]

'. . . bring together men and women of ability and promise from industry, commerce, the trade unions, and all forms of the public service . . .

'. . . provide a course of studies which investigates the principles and techniques of organization and administration in civil life . . . and

'. . . foster understanding between those who carry responsibility in different spheres by giving them the opportunity to interchange ideas and experience at an age when their views have been formed but not fixed.'

The college sessions last three months. The first session opened with forty-five members; by the ninth applications for places had become sufficiently numerous to plan permanently for sixty, which was regarded as the optimum number. This total is made up of approximately 50 per cent members from private industry and commerce; 10 per cent from each of the Civil Service, the nationalized undertakings, and banking, insurance and finance; and 5 per cent from each of local government, the fighting services, and oversea concerns. Selection also takes into account variety of experience within these groups, the geographical distribution of the candidates, and the size of the firms in which they work.

[1] Quoted from the college Handbook.

OPPORTUNITIES FOR ADULTS

Most of the work at the college is done in syndicates of ten members, each made up to give the utmost variety of experience. The course consists of four parts. In Part I members give, first, personal experiences in administration, after which the syndicates examine issues common to all spheres of civilian employment. In Part II matters within the control of a single executive authority and in Part III those calling for action by two or more, are surveyed. In Part IV the conclusions previously reached are applied to specific problems. This programme is varied by visits from guest speakers, and by members to industrial, commercial and professional concerns.

An opportunity of a very different kind was offered, from January 1946 onwards, by the National Council of Y.M.C.A.s to men in industry or commerce who occupied, or might be expected in the future to occupy, managerial or administrative posts. This was a full university term at Cambridge. The students live in Cheshunt College, an old-established theological college belonging to the Congregational denomination. They arrange with the tutor a programme of studies, the choice including English literature, history, psychology, economics, philosophy, and theology. The college offers them various lecture courses and guides their work, and by arrangement with the university they are admitted to university lecture courses and other activities. The aim is 'to enable them to widen their interests, to take stock of their ideas and examine them in the light of experience gained in living and working in fresh surroundings along with others engaged in the pursuit of learning'.[1] I visited these courses on several occasions and was left in no doubt about how valuable the experience was; students and their employers were unanimous in their praise.

It was not long before the demand for places exceeded the number available, and by 1952 about thirty firms and organizations were sending students. In that year the Y.M.C.A. made

[1] Quoted from the prospectus of the courses at Durham, but precisely applicable to Cambridge.

OPPORTUNITIES FOR ADULTS

similar courses available at the College of the Venerable Bede in Durham University. The association had also for years been meeting the needs of promising young apprentices and trainees in industrial or commercial employment at two residential colleges, Glyn House at Kingsgate near Broadstairs in Kent, and Coleg y Fro at Rhoose in Glamorganshire. At these colleges courses varying in length from a week-end to a month were offered; and again I can testify from first-hand acquaintance to the value these were to students. In some cases, especially as a result of one of the longer courses, nothing less than a transformation was effected.

NO COUNTY COLLEGES

Such opportunities for young people were the more valuable because one of the unrealized hopes of these years was the County College. It is probably true to say that when Section 43[1] was written into the Education Act, 1944, everyone anticipated that it would be brought into operation within a relatively short time. This expectation only gradually faded.

In October 1945 the Ministry of Education published an admirable booklet entitled *Youth's Opportunity* which dealt in detail with the buildings, organization, curriculum, and other activities proposed for county colleges. As late as 1947 the then Minister of Education, Mr. George Tomlinson, was declaring in public speeches that 'county colleges must be the next major reform, because the whole structure of further education depends on accustoming young workers to study and earn a living at the same time, and on getting industry to accept this as good practice'. But even then he was having to admit that 'everything depends upon accommodation'.

[1] On and after such date as His Majesty may by Order in Council determine, not later than three years after the date of commencement of this Part of this Act, it shall be the duty of every local education authority to establish and maintain county colleges . . . for young persons who are not in full-time attendance at any school . . .

OPPORTUNITIES FOR ADULTS

It was not, I think, until 1949 that hope was generally abandoned of an early introduction of universal compulsory part-time education. But by then it had become perfectly clear to everyone, except the inevitable few who remained incorrigibly air-borne, that to implement fully the 1944 Act was going to take far longer than most people had imagined during the over-optimistic years directly after the war. In 1948 people were still seriously debating whether the raising of compulsory school age to 16 or the enforcement of compulsory part-time education should come first: the assumption being that one or the other would shortly be accomplished. By 1949 the debate had become academic; one was compelled by the facts of the nation's situation to admit, most reluctantly but quite finally, that neither reform could be carried through within the next few years.

In 1949 a senior officer of the Ministry of Education gave me figures which showed that to provide only the barely necessary accommodation to house the increasing school population would take all the materials and labour which the Ministry could hope to procure for primary and secondary education until the end of 1955. After that, he argued, and I could not but agree, must first come the replacement of 'all-age' and other out-of-date or dilapidated school buildings, so that the reorganization of the school system into primary and secondary sections could be completed. Until that was accomplished there could not be truly 'secondary education for all'. To complete reorganization, he estimated, would take a further five years. Not before 1960, therefore, could even a start upon county colleges be expected.

By 1952 few people expected to see universal part-time education in county colleges for many years. Not, I think, because there was any waning of desire to see this reform effected; on the contrary, many people—employers in particular—who were hostile or indifferent to it in 1945 had come to see how desirable, indeed necessary, it was. No: simply because adverse circumstances had revealed starkly what more propitious times might have concealed: that with the best will in the world the effecting of large-scale reorganizations has to be reckoned in terms of decades, if not generations, rather than of years.

When our great-grandchildren come to write the history of the mid-twentieth century they may criticize us for not having spread our resources more thinly over a wider area. They may say that instead of spending huge sums to provide, and equip superbly, palatial schools, as we did between 1946 and 1949, we ought to have had the sense to build as economically as we were doing in 1952, and that then we should have had materials and labour to spare for county colleges. After all, they may point out, the Board of Education did warn us in 1939 of the danger of neglecting the working adolescent, and so, if memory be carried still further back, did the Lewis Committee in 1916.

In principle, I agree; but I cannot convince myself that the small amount we might have saved on the building of primary and secondary schools would have gone any noticeable way towards providing county colleges. Even if it had, there would have been no teachers to staff the colleges, except at the cost of denying them to the schools; and with all the efforts that were made these were still gravely short of teachers in 1952.

There may yet prove to be something to be said for the slower—but, I feel, surer—progress we have made towards universal part-time education by way of a voluntary movement. This will in time embrace all the young people in the land; it will have carried public support with it all the way; and its gradual progress may have enabled teachers and administrators to learn how to educate the working boy and girl, a matter about which as yet they know less than about how to give secondary education to all children. We may later be thankful that harsh circumstances forced us to take a course which, though disappointingly slow, was fundamentally the wisest.

AGRICULTURAL EDUCATION

Until very recent years agricultural education lagged badly behind other forms of vocational education, and it could not even in 1952 be said to have anything like caught up. The farmer is traditionally reluctant to be taught—or to have his sons and employees taught. Yet between the first and second world wars a considerable organization for agricultural and horticultural education was built up in England and Wales. In 1939 this was functioning in three well-defined sections. Advanced education was being given in seven agricultural colleges and seven university departments of agriculture, and more elementary practical instruction in seventeen county Farm Institutes. Moreover, the country had been divided into thirteen provinces, in each of which a research centre had been established, at which a corps of specialist advisers was available to give expert help to farmers, whether in response to individual requests or by arranging courses and conferences.

During the second world war this organization largely disintegrated. The university departments of agriculture certainly continued to offer their normal courses (though perpetually harassed by losing staff), but the agricultural colleges during the earlier years and the farm institutes throughout were diverted to training volunteers for the Women's Land Army. Most of the specialist advisers were transferred to service with the County War Agricultural Executive Committees, which as time went on made also increasing demands upon the staffs in the university departments, agricultural colleges and farm institutes.

As in so many other areas of the national life, advantage was taken of this temporary disruption of the normal services to subject them to critical review. In July 1941 the Minister of Agriculture appointed a committee, under the chairmanship of the late Lord Luxmoore, 'to examine the present system of agricultural education in England and Wales and to make recommendations for improving and developing it after the war'. The committee's report,[1] published in January 1943, found little wrong with either the nature or the quality of the educational facilities provided, but thought their organization defective in three respects:

(i) The absence of any authority charged with the positive duty of providing any form of agricultural education.

(ii) The number of different authorities which provided agricultural education.

(iii) The diversity of the sources and available means of finance.

To remedy these defects the committee recommended that there be set up:

'A central statutory authority (which we call the National Council for Agricultural Education) charged with the positive duty of providing, at the cost of the National Exchequer, for the different branches of agricultural education and with the necessary powers to enable it to perform this duty. This council should be so constituted that it is outside the Ministry of Agriculture, but is under the control of the Minister who should be answerable for it to Parliament.'

The Government, however, rejected this idea of an all-embracing authority on the grounds that agricultural education should not be thus completely divorced from the statutory system of public education. Instead, it decided to combine the previous provincial and county advisory services in a national service under the Minister of Agriculture, who would also be responsible for advanced agricultural education, and to leave agricultural education at farm institute level and below, as before, in the hands of the local education authorities, but making its provision mandatory upon them. (It had before been permissive only.) Two committees, both under the chairmanship of Dr. T. Loveday, then Vice-Chancellor of Bristol

[1] *Report of the Committee on Post-War Agricultural Education in England and Wales.* Cmd. 6433. H.M. Stationery Office, 1943.

University (who had been a member of the Luxmoore Committee), and including an element of common membership, were set up in July 1944 to advise on post-war policy. Their respective terms of reference were:

(i) To consider the character and extent of the need for higher agricultural education in England and Wales and to make recommendations as to the facilities which should be provided to meet the needs.

(ii) To advise on all aspects of agricultural education and particularly on the educational policy and methods of training to be adopted at farm institutes.

The committee on higher education reported[1] in December 1945. The other, which was still in being in 1952, produced a series of reports, beginning with one in April 1945 on the *Provision in Secondary Schools of Courses preparatory to Agricultural Employment*. In November 1947 came *Agricultural and Horticultural Institutes*, and in June 1949 *The Provision of Part-time Instruction by local education authorities for agriculturists, horticulturists and domestic producers*.

The two committees had agreed that agricultural education should continue to be provided at the same three institutional levels—university, college, and farm institute—and progress followed those lines. Among its notable features was a large increase in the number of farm institutes, of which there were thirty-seven in 1952. This increase was, unfortunately, somewhat in advance of public opinion among the farming community; many of the institutes found it difficult to fill all their places. This unfortunate situation may be eased in the future by the success of agriculturally biased courses in secondary schools. Especially should it be so when, as in Somerset, a secondary technical school for agriculture is established adjacent to and working in close co-operation with the county farm institute. This experiment, begun in September 1952,

[1] *Higher Agricultural Education in England and Wales*. Cmd. 6728. H.M. Stationery Office, 1946.

will be watched with closest interest, particularly as Brymore is a boarding school, and so able to attract, as it has already done, pupils from every part of the county and beyond. Another factor, too, should help matters: the projected national apprenticeship scheme for young farm workers. But up to the end of 1952 this had not come into being.

'CULTURAL, TRAINING AND RECREATIVE'

It will be recalled that Section 41 of the Education Act, 1944, laid upon the local education authorities the duty of providing, 'for persons over compulsory school age', not only 'full-time and part-time education' but also:

'(*b*) leisure-time occupation, in such organized cultural training and recreative activities as are suited to their requirements . . .'

In Circular 61 (9th August 1945) the Ministry emphasized that 'the development of non-vocational work of this kind . . . is an important function which local education authorities are called upon to discharge'.

Section 53 of the Act emphasizes the size of the field which the authorities were expected to cover. By that section they were empowered to provide (or assist in providing) for adults as well as children, 'camps, holiday classes, playing fields, play centres . . . playgrounds, gymnasiums, and swimming baths', and to 'organize games, expeditions and other activities'. To that list the Government had in 1944 added community centres. All this in addition to a multitudinous variety of indoor activities, which ranged from classes in philosophy to instruction in dancing and the repair of household furniture.

There is no doubt that immediately after the war there was a genuine, and widespread, desire to provide greatly expanded and improved facilities for the education of adults—using the term 'education' in the sense of the generously broad phrase in Section 41: 'cultural training and recreative activities'. In particular, there was a general desire that opportunities for education comparable with those which many of them had enjoyed in the Services should be available in civil life to the men and women being demobilized.

'During the past five years there has been built up in the Services a system of education for adults in the broadest sense of the term . . . such as has never before been attempted, and covering a wide range of interests and activities . . .

'. . . very large numbers of men and women have been introduced for the first time to new interests, whether in current affairs, the foundations of the British and democratic way of life, or in subjects with a vocational purpose or of a purely recreative character. *Many have been awakened to new ideas about the need for thinking and to new possibilities, previously unrealized, of the development within themselves, and in co-operation with others, of resources for the fuller appreciation of life and enjoyment of leisure.*' (Italics mine.)

'There will thus be presented to the education service in the sphere of adult education', said the circular, 'what is at once a new problem and a new opportunity'.[1] It is among the major tragedies of the post-war years that this opportunity was let slip.

The opportunity was there, beyond a doubt. The sentence in Circular 57 which I have italicized contains no element of over-statement or wishful thinking; I talked with hundreds of serving or recently demobilized men and women, of every rank from private to full general, during those months immediately after the war, and I can never forget the intense longing—amounting to a physical hunger—which so many had for some means to satisfy their desire for mental and spiritual sustenance.

No one was to blame that this uniquely magnificent opportunity was lost: or, if you like, everyone was. The public authorities were driven off their feet by other tasks; voluntary organizations could get neither men nor materials to do the

[1] Ministry of Education Circular 57, *Demobilization and Adult Education*, dated 9th July 1945.

job; the demobilized men and women became caught up in the preoccupations of working and domestic life; commercialized entertainment was at hand, promptly and efficiently, to offer them glittering palliatives; and in a very short time everyone was too busy, or too tired, or too anxious, or too preoccupied with other matters to bother much about adult education any more. The overriding problem was how we were going to live at all, not how we were going to live 'the fuller life', as the more earnest adult educationists put it in their horrible jargon.

Not everything was lost; in fact, did one not realize how immense was the opportunity one could feel highly gratified at the advance that was made. The numbers enrolling for courses of liberal studies spurted upwards. In 1946–7 the university extra-mural departments and the other Responsible Bodies[1] provided some 6,000 classes for 138,000 students, as compared with 3,000 classes containing 60,000 students in 1938–9. That this increase was no flash in the pan was evidenced by the fact that for the next three years the number of classes rose by about 1,000 a year. It was still rising, though at a much slower rate, in 1951, when 8,090 classes were provided for 162,850 students—nearly three times as many as before the war, but even so a pitifully small proportion of the adult population. A great mass of indifference remained.

That this type of leisure-time adult education was attracting new elements in the population was, however, clear by the marked preference for the shorter kinds of course—the sessional and terminal—and the more informal types of subject and instruction. The number of three-year tutorial classes[2] provided

---

[1] A 'Responsible Body' is a body of persons, not a statutory authority nor a body exercising powers on behalf of such an authority, which is recognized and grant aided by the Ministry of Education as responsible for the provision of liberal adult education. All the universities are Responsible Bodies, and so is the Workers' Educational Association (W.E.A.).

[2] A tutorial class comprises seventy-two two-hour meetings spread over three years. A sessional class normally comprises twenty-four meetings, a terminal twelve.

by the Workers' Educational Association and the University Extra-Mural Departments increased; by 1951 it had nearly reached 1,000, but the relative increase was much less than that of the shorter classes, and tutorial work constituted in 1952 a considerably smaller proportion of all extra-mural and W.E.A. work than it ever did before the war. This was a cause for much concern to one section of adult educationists, of whom Mr. (later Professor) S. G. Raybould, Director of the Extra-Mural Department of Leeds University, became the principal spokesman.

'If the universities cease to be interested in whether their extra-mural work is of university standard or not, and devote a large proportion of their resources to organizing and to work of an elementary character', wrote Mr. Raybould,[1] 'the outcome can only be disastrous—for the W.E.A., for extra-mural work itself, and for the student'. It would be disastrous for the W.E.A. 'because its claim to a special position among voluntary bodies concerned with adult education . . . can only be upheld so long as it can show that its class work is distinctive by reason of particularly high quality'. It would be disastrous for extra-mural work 'because the best scholars and teachers in the universities will cease to be interested in it, and its reputation, inside and outside the universities' walls, will decline'. And, 'worst of all', it would be disastrous for the students, 'who instead of receiving education at the highest level practicable for part-time students, will be put off with a greatly inferior substitute'.

Mr. Raybould and those of his mind saw decadence in the trend towards shorter courses; students, they thought, were crowding into these because they were unwilling to face the more rigorous intellectual disciplines of the tutorial class. On the other hand, there was a body of opinion which believed that the need for tutorial classes was diminishing, and would con-

[1] *The W.E.A. The Next Phase.* By S. G. Raybould. Published by the Workers' Educational Association, 1949, p. 64.

tinue to diminish, because, as a result of the Education Act, 1944, whereas formerly many men and women of ability but lacking means had had to seek education of university standard through tutorial classes, henceforth such men and women would be almost certain to pass through the university in their youth. But, argued those of this opinion, there would be an increasing number of young people coming out of the schools, and in particular out of the secondary modern school, who, while intellectually not capable of work of three-year tutorial standard, would wish to continue their cultural education at a somewhat lower level. For these the sessional and terminal courses were admirably designed.

Neither party to this argument had convinced the other by 1952. Nor could the impartial observer come down wholly on one side or the other; there were too many other factors involved beside those cited above to allow of any certain judgement from the not very conclusive evidence of figures. All that was certain was that the *pro rata* demand for shorter and lighter courses steadily increased, and showed every sign of continuing to do so.

An extreme illustration of this was the sudden emergence of a novel and most attractive institution: the short-term residential college for adult education offering, in the main, courses lasting over a week-end only. There had been occasional experiments before the war with brief residential courses open to the general public, and the study week-end was, of course, no novelty to scholars. But it was probably the multiplicity of short training courses, many of them residential, held during the war which prompted the thought of carrying the idea over into civil life. No one in particular seems to have been the 'onlie begetter' of the short-course residential college; it sprang up almost simultaneously in different parts of the country from 1945 onwards, and under both private and public auspices, though mainly the latter. By 1947 there were eleven colleges, and by 1952 twenty-five, through which passed in that year more than 70,000 people, from all ranks of society and every type of occupation.

Most of the colleges are housed in spacious country houses, usually surrounded by ample, and often beautiful, grounds. Some of these houses, such as Attingham Park, in Shropshire, which is National Trust property, Dillington House in Somerset, and Grantley Hall in the West Riding, have distinguished architectural features; others, like Ashridge in Hertfordshire—by far the largest—a history of interest and consequence. Almost all have a gracious and dignified atmosphere, which is often enriched by noble rooms, internal decorations by master craftsmen, or works of art left by previous owners. That is one reason why they attract; to live, if only for a week-end, in one of the 'stately homes of England' is in itself a liberal education. A second, perhaps more plebeian but certainly most important, reason is that the present owners of the colleges, whether they be local education authorities or private bodies, do their utmost to make their guests thoroughly comfortable. 'A college like this', one warden said to me, 'survives on its food, its beds and its armchairs'.

There is much truth in those words. The main problem the colleges had to face during their earlier years was that of adjusting income and expenditure. If students were charged high fees they would not—in many cases could not—come; if the charges were modest the college's financial deficit grew mountain high. Some local education authorities were at first inclined to regard the colleges as a costly luxury, and until it became generally accepted that the colleges could most of them never be fully self-supporting the lives of more than a few were in jeopardy.

Most of the colleges are maintained by local education authorities, which are generally the owners of the property. One college, Burton Manor, in the Wirral, is maintained by six authorities: the county boroughs of Birkenhead, Bootle, Liverpool, and Wallasey, and the counties of Cheshire and

Lancashire. The Wedgwood Memorial College at Barlaston in Staffordshire is run by a joint committee representing the Staffordshire, Stoke-on-Trent and Burton-on-Trent local education authorities, the North Staffordshire district of the W.E.A., the Oxford University delegacy for Extra-Mural studies, and the University College of North Staffordshire. Westham House in Warwickshire is supported by Birmingham University, which also maintains, at Primrose Hill, in Birmingham, a residential centre for more advanced studies. Holly Royde, also a city college, is part of the Extra-Mural Department of Manchester University. Denman College in Berkshire is the property of the National Federation of Women's Institutes, Ashridge of an independent council, Stoke House near Bletchley and Pendley Manor in Hertfordshire of private individuals.

While the main activity of almost all the colleges is the provision of week-end courses, they all offer courses of somewhat longer duration, and the trend during the years under review was to increase both the duration and the number of such longer courses. By 1952 courses occupying the inside of a week (Monday to Friday) were common, and there were others extending over a full week, ten days, a fortnight, and, in a few cases, as long as a month. Several of the larger colleges had developed the practice of holding simultaneously two courses, generally of dissimilar length; this had the incidental advantage of bringing together at meals and in social intercourse groups of people with different interests.

Courses fell into two categories, open and closed; for the former any member of the public might apply, while the latter were reserved to members of specific groups, usually organizations which hired the college facilities for the duration of the course. All the colleges except Stoke House offered both open and closed courses; in most the former were more numerous. The range of topics covered was almost illimitable, except that in the first instance strictly vocational courses were excluded.

This rule was later abandoned, to such an extent in some cases that one acute observer[1] feared they might become 'a mere tool of industrial training or administrative bureaucracy'.

To give an idea of the variety of courses, those held at one college in a single month included 'The Countryside in Winter', 'Supervisory Management', 'Youth Leadership', 'Handicrafts', and 'Clear Thinking, Speaking and Writing'. At another, five consecutive courses—all open—were 'International Trade and Finance', 'Painting and Sculpture', 'Crime and the Criminal', 'Modern Europe', and 'The Management of Industry'. A third offered in successive weeks 'Nineteenth Century Social History', 'Science and Human Progress', 'Stars, Planets and the Zodiac', and 'The Mystery of Bird Migration'.

By 1952 several of the colleges had developed a marked bias in favour of particular types of course. Burton Manor, Grantley Hall, Pendley, and Urchfont Manor (Wiltshire) had all achieved something more than a local reputation for courses on industrial topics. Missenden Abbey in Buckinghamshire was giving much of its time to parties of school teachers and other professional people from Germany—a generous and pleasing gesture on the part of a local education authority. Debden House in Essex, run by the East Ham authority, was taking advantage of its proximity to Epping Forest to offer series of courses on the history, people, flora and fauna of this famous woodland. Westham House, similarly, making admirable use of its rural and riverine setting in the Shakespeare country (it is on the banks of the River Avon between Warwick and Stratford), was specializing on Shakespeariana and country life. Belstead House in Suffolk was devoting its attention mainly to meeting the professional needs of its teachers, and Woolley Hall in the West Riding entirely so. Denman College was catering exclusively for the practical and cultural needs of members

---

[1] Guy Hunter, warden of Urchfont Manor and later of Grantley Hall, in *Residential Colleges, Some New Developments in British Adult Education.* Published in the United States by The Fund for Adult Education, 1952.

of Women's Institutes, and Primrose Hill for those of professional people and specialists. Holly Royde concentrated mainly on the study of society. Ashridge, because of its size, included among its activities the accommodation of international gatherings. Stoke House was unique in being the only college devoted entirely to craftwork. All its courses were 'open'.

It would be unwise as yet to attempt to predict what the place or the contribution of the short-term residential college will ultimately prove to be; all one can say at present is that it appears to have established itself firmly as a new and attractive institution which is undoubtedly drawing into the sphere of liberal adult education many thousands of people who would never have been persuaded to undertake more formal studies in a specifically academic atmosphere. It has, of course, many dangers to avoid, and not least those presented by too easy success.

Mr. Guy Hunter[1] has clearly analysed some of these dangers:

'. . . the maintenance of ideals and standards is critical. It is the occupational disease of all educational movements, when faced with difficulty, to relax standards and popularize, and it is the surest sign of coming failure.'[2]

Writing in 1952, he felt that some of the colleges were succumbing to that disease.

'At present the very rapid stream of students through the colleges is being bought at the expense of quality—sessions inadequately prepared for, students left to the mercies of a complete stranger who comes by train to lecture for a day and then disappears, staff living on nervous energy and idealism beyond the point of efficiency[3] . . .

'. . . the tendency to run more and more courses of shorter and shorter duration, to overwork the staff, to admit trivial work and be content with trivial results, is too well-marked to neglect and too dangerous to the future of the colleges to excuse.'[4]

So, while he is fully conscious of the great possibilities which lie before the colleges—and no man did more in these years to

[1] *Op. cit.*, 25.   [2] p. 51.   [3] p. 56.   [4] p. 57.

realize them—Mr. Hunter is forced to conclude that 'It is at present an open question whether the colleges will degenerate into a mere facility for existing work or will live on to make a real new contribution of their own.'[1]

Important as these colleges may be, they constitute but one element in a much larger growth of residential education for adults which has spread with amazing rapidity almost from nothing since the war. Every educational establishment in the country which could offer bed and board was in 1952, and had been for some years previously, besieged with applications to let its accommodation during holidays and week-ends. Some had every available day booked up for as much as two or three years ahead. Hotels at seasonal resorts were being similarly inundated with inquiries. Many large industrial, commercial and professional organizations had their own residential training centres, such as Ashorne Hill near Leamington, the property of the British Iron and Steel Federation. So, too, had voluntary organizations. Those of the Y.M.C.A. have been mentioned previously. The Y.W.C.A., Scouts, Guides, Boys' Brigade, and the National Association of Boys' Clubs were among others who had residential centres for young people. The Central Council of Physical Recreation had established three for the training of adults and adolescents. There was every indication that adult education in a residential setting had come to stay, and on a relatively large scale.

Mention must be made of one unique institution in a rather different field: Wilton Park. Financed and administered by the Foreign Office, this began in January 1946 to give to selected German prisoners of war courses illustrating the democratic way of life. In January 1947 civilians from Germany were also admitted. In June 1948 the courses for prisoners ceased, and between then and December 1952 over 2,000 German men and women, all engaged in public affairs, came from Germany to be the guests of Wilton Park. Housed since January 1950 in a

[1] p. 56.

beautiful Elizabethan Manor near Steyning in Sussex, Wilton Park has become a vitally important bridge between British and German public opinion. It enjoys almost complete autonomy, brings the most eminent people in British life to its sessions and conducts, on a basis of equality between the nations, impartial discussions of all aspects of British and German life and policy.

Non-residential adult education centres maintained by local education authorities also made their appearance here and there, especially in large towns, but though in individual cases they were great successes their progress did not compare with that of the residential centres. An allied movement, probably in the long run much more important, was the gradual transformation of many technical colleges into general colleges of further education (often under that title) by the introduction of courses in humane subjects, and the giving to the colleges a more social atmosphere by the provision of refectories, lounges, reading rooms and concert halls.

Far too little could be done in these respects even during the years when shortages of labour and materials were not completely prohibitive. Early in 1952 the work was brought to an almost complete stop. In Circular 245 (4th February 1952) the Ministry of Education announced that 'until further notice building work at community centres, village halls, youth clubs and other institutions for youth and adult welfare must be restricted to maintenance and jobs costing less than £1,000 for the adaptation and repair of existing premises'. For an unknown period, then, liberal adult education can expect from the public purse no addition to its material resources. It remains to be seen whether the impetus given to it during the years of expansion will be sufficient to justify the term being applied in 1952 to the years ahead: 'years of consolidation', or whether there will be, as many fear, a gradual loss of enthusiasm and a consequent diminution in numbers and facilities.

Chapter Five

UNIVERSITY EXPANSION

As I recorded in my previous volume,[1] between 1939 and 1945 the British universities were largely diverted from their normal purposes to serve the war effort in a wide variety of ways. The end of war found them with greatly depleted staffs, a much decreased and very unbalanced student population, and short of many essential buildings which had either been taken over by Government departments or destroyed by enemy action.

By 1944 only 68 per cent of full-time university teachers were still at their posts. The total number of students had fallen from 50,000 to 35,500, a drop of 28 per cent. Those figures, however, disguise rather than illuminate the true position. The number of women students had actually increased by 13 per cent, while that of men had fallen by 41 per cent, and of men in the Arts Faculties by 76 per cent. Moreover, most of the men in attendance were taking shortened courses only, many of no more than one year's duration.

Most of the universities, happily, had either escaped air-raid damage or been relatively lightly scarred. But Bristol and Liverpool had suffered severely, and London extensively. Here, heavy damage had been done at University College, Bedford College, Birkbeck College, St. Bartholomew's Hospital Medical College, the London School of Hygiene and Tropical Medicine, the London School of Medicine for Women, and King's College of Household and Social Science; and few of the

[1] *Education in Transition*, pp. 137–44.

buildings belonging to the many other institutions attached to this university had gone unscathed.

London University, moreover, was still partially evacuated. Though some of its schools had remained, in whole or in part, in the city throughout the war, and many had returned (again, in whole or in part) before its close, the cessation of hostilities found large numbers of its staffs and students widely dispersed, and its main buildings in Bloomsbury still firmly occupied by the Ministry of Information.

But while London was in particularly desperate case, all the universities and university colleges were, to a large degree, temporarily drained of their strength and diminished in their resources. What most of them really needed—it would have been ideal could it have happened—was a period of quiet recuperation, in which to recall their scattered staffs and fill up the gaps in their ranks, build up again gradually their student population, balancing it as they went, reclaim those buildings that had been requisitioned and restore those that had been wrecked, and—in the last analysis most important of all—to reconsider in tranquillity their aims and functions in the light of greatly altered circumstances and to replan their organization and remake their curricula accordingly.

This was not to be; indeed, could not have been. Total war allows to academic institutions no more than to any others a breathing space; on the contrary, it piles up for them rather more than for most an accumulation of immediately urgent tasks.

However grievous their material and academic problems, the moment the war was over the universities had to expect knocking at their doors a six-years' backlog of men and (to some extent) women who in normal circumstances would have come up between 1939 and 1945. That by itself would have meant a steep rise in the number of students during the years immediately following the war. But in the event this was to prove a minor element only in the vast host with which the universities were confronted. For national foresight and public sentiment had joined forces to demand that the doors of the universities be thrown open to ability much more widely than ever before, so wide indeed that literally no one judged capable of profiting from university education should be denied it.

No one knew quite what this would mean in numbers, though during the war varied estimates had been made. As early as mid-1943 a Committee on Post-War University Education set up by the British Association for the Advancement of Science was talking in terms of 'an immediate advance of 50 per cent on the 1938–9 figures for the universities of England and Wales'.[1] A report by the Association of University Teachers published early in 1944 suggested the same figure. These were among the more modest estimates. The Parliamentary and Scientific Committee, in a report on 'Scientific Research and the Universities in Post-War Britain', published in October 1943, anticipated that the universities would have to produce ultimately something like three times as many scientists and technologists. And as, said the Committee, 'There can be no question of reducing the numbers in other subjects', the country might have to look forward to 'an ultimate doubling of the total numbers enjoying university education'.

It was recognized by everyone that no such expansion could be financed out of the universities' own resources, and that consequently greatly increased State aid would have to be made available. Here again estimates varied. The British Association Committee declared that 'The Treasury grant should be at once doubled after the war.' The Parliamentary and Scientific Committee went much further; it suggested that the grant should be raised from £2,250,000[2] to six or seven million pounds'.

The universities had early become convinced of the necessity

---

[1] Note on a Universities' Advisory Council, p. 1. See also the Committee's Report *On University Finance in Great Britain*, July 1943, p. 6.

[2] The Treasury grant had been stabilized during the war at the 1938–9 figure of £2,149,000.

UNIVERSITY EXPANSION

to expand. But before they could make any definite plans they had to know what such expansion might be expected to cost, and what financial assistance from public funds they could reckon on. Accordingly, in June 1943 the Committee of Vice-Chancellors and Principals, which during the war acted on behalf of the universities as a whole in their negotiations with Government departments, asked the University Grants Committee 'to set on foot a review of the financial implications which national policy would require the universities to undertake, both in the immediate future and in the next ten or twenty years'.[1] They suggested that particular attention should be directed to:

(i) the capital and maintenance costs of new lands and buildings;

(ii) the cost of maintaining adequate teaching establishments adequately paid;

(iii) the cost of maintaining and developing fundamental research.

The Committee further suggested that if the universities were fully to meet national needs after the war the Government would have to make them non-recurrent grants for capital expenditure 'on a scale not hitherto contemplated' and increase greatly its contribution to their income.

In response to this appeal the University Grants Committee in November 1943 asked the universities and university colleges to submit statements about their proposed development policy during the first ten years after the war, with estimates of the expenditure, both capital and current, which this would involve. These statements were presented early in 1944, and in January 1945, following an exhaustive examination of the proposals (in the course of which several were considerably altered), the U.G.C. advised the Treasury to increase the annual grant to the universities during each of the first two years after the

[1] *University Development from 1935 to 1947*, Report of the University Grants Committee, H.M. Stationery Office, 1948, p. 76.

war from £2,149,000 to £4,149,000. In addition, the Committee advised that in each of these years a further sum of £1,000,000 be granted towards meeting the cost of developing medical education along the lines recommended by the Goodenough Committee,[1] whose recommendations the Government had already accepted.

This Committee, which reported in May 1944, had proposed radical reforms in the system of medical education. Among these were:

(i) Undergraduate medical education to be conducted only in university medical schools;

(ii) Immediate increase of the number of students at existing medical schools below an economical size. An entry of about a hundred students a year was recommended.

(iii) Co-education to become the normal practice in all medical schools, and the payment of Treasury grant to be conditional upon the admission of a reasonable proportion of women students.

(iv) All clinical departments in medical schools to be headed by full-time professors, paid salaries sufficient to obviate any need to supplement these by other earnings.

(v) Part-time clinical teachers to be paid salaries, not lecture fees.

(vi) The teaching hospitals to receive Treasury grant towards expenditure on teaching and research.

(vii) The British Postgraduate Medical School at Hammersmith to be reconstituted as a federal organization embracing a number of hospitals.

The Goodenough Committee had estimated that to carry out these reforms a capital expenditure of some £5,000,000 would be required and an addition to the income of medical schools which would amount within ten years to between £1,750,000 and £2,500,000 a year, at pre-war values.

[1] *Medical Schools*. Report of the Inter-Departmental Committee (Chairman, Sir William Goodenough, Bt.). H.M. Stationery Office, 1944.

UNIVERSITY EXPANSION

The Treasury accepted the U.G.C.'s recommendations, and a public announcement to this effect was made by the then Chancellor of the Exchequer, Sir John Anderson, in April 1945. In May the University Grants Committee invited all the universities in Great Britain and the University Colleges of Exeter, Nottingham and Southampton to submit estimates of the additional number of students they felt they could make provision for during the years immediately ahead.

The modern universities and the university colleges responded in generous fashion; altogether, they were prepared to increase their student numbers by 86 per cent within ten years. Oxford and Cambridge were of a very different opinion; no increase in their numbers, they thought, was practicable if their academic standards were to be maintained.

It should not be assumed that this *non possumus* from Oxford and Cambridge indicated either a purblind conservatism or any lack of appreciation of the nation's needs. They were indeed keenly sensitive of them. But to both the ancient universities expansion presented peculiar and formidable difficulties. Their academic staffs had been far more seriously depleted by war demands than those of other universities and the university colleges. Their medieval buildings and precincts did not lend themselves easily to the provision of additional accommodation. To expand lodging facilities was hardly less difficult; both the university towns are relatively small and both lie in sparsely populated rural areas. Moreover, both Oxford and Cambridge were in 1939 more than twice as large as any other English university except London, which can hardly be regarded as typical. Cambridge, indeed, with 5,931 students, was almost three times as large.[1]

During the preparation of these post-war development plans there had been much discussion about the optimum size of a university. In this the English preference for small academic

[1] Only Manchester (2,108) and Liverpool (2,055) exceeded 2,000 in the academic year 1938-9.

institutions had been clearly manifest; few people thought in terms of universities as large as Oxford and Cambridge, and many were inclined to agree with Leeds, which in the proposals it submitted to the University Grants Committee in 1944 asserted that 'a size of much more than 3,000 students' would prejudice the idea of a university as a community. Not a few people preferred even smaller numbers than this.

In the aggregate the increase in numbers offered in 1945 by the universities and university colleges amounted to some 45 per cent. Then, in May 1946, appeared the 'Barlow' Report.[1] This said bluntly that the country needed many more highly trained scientists, and that it needed them quickly. In 1945, said the Report, the tally was 55,000; by 1955 it should be at least 90,000. The immediate aim should be to double the annual output of scientists, that is, in round figures to produce some 5,000 a year, of which the university share would be 3,500, in place of the pre-war average annual output of 2,500. In addition, the universities should continue to be responsible for training 'a high proportion of the nation's first-class technologists'.

Moreover, added the Committee, it had been informed that there was need for a 'very substantial increase' in the number of graduates in the humanities, languages and the fine arts. The Committee would welcome this, and it would particularly 'deprecate any attempt to meet the increased demand for scientists and technologists at the expense of students of other subjects'.[2]

The Barlow Committee submitted no figure for the increase in the number of art students. But it was widely assumed that this should be broadly proportionate to that of the scientists. Even on the assumption that it might be slightly smaller, it

[1] *Scientific Manpower*. Report of the Committee appointed by the Lord President of the Council (Chairman, Sir Alan Barlow, Bt.) Cmd. 6824. H.M. Stationery Office 1946.
[2] p. 11.

was clear that the British universities and university colleges as a whole were now faced with the demand to increase their student numbers by about the proportion which their most forthcoming group—the civic universities and the university colleges—was prepared to undertake, that is, by about 85 per cent within ten years.

The challenge was accepted; and the resultant action far exceeded the promise. Within two years—not ten—the number of students of science and technology at the universities had been doubled, and that of other students had risen by 50 per cent. In the academic year 1943-4 the total number of students was 37,500. By 1946-7 it had soared to 63,000, by 1947-8 to nearly 77,000 and by 1949-50—the peak year to date—to 85,421. Even in 1950-1, when total numbers in Great Britain fell by 107, the number in the English universities increased by over 1,000. In 1951-2, when numbers again decreased slightly, it seemed likely that they were becoming stable.

To this great increase the civic universities and the university colleges had, as they promised, contributed most. By 1950-1 only Leeds, Liverpool and Reading were less than double the size they were in 1938-9. The growth of some of the smaller institutions was, to put it mildly, spectacular. Leicester University College, previously a private establishment with fewer than a hundred students (eighty-two in 1938-9), was in 1945 put on the Treasury grant list, and by 1950-1 had jumped to 730. The University College of Hull, similarly grant-aided from 1945, increased its numbers even more largely. Before the war these had never exceeded 200 (168 in 1938-9) and during it they fell to about eighty. By 1950-1 they were 917. Both these colleges received Royal Charters as University Colleges in 1951.

Southampton University College (268 to 980) and Nottingham University College (582 to 2,112) almost quadrupled in size, and Sheffield University (769 to 2,024) nearly trebled. Altogether, 'Redbrick', as Bruce Truscot dubbed[1] the modern

[1] *Redbrick University* by Bruce Truscot. Faber, 1943.

universities, which had offered to increase its student population by 86 per cent within ten years, actually increased it by nearly 130 per cent in five.

This breathtakingly rapid expansion naturally created problems in every part of university life, and outside it. To some of these reference will be made later. Because it was undertaken deliberately to meet specific national needs, and was financed almost wholly out of public funds, it also raised an issue of national policy of fundamental importance: the relationship between the universities and the State.

The British universities and university colleges have always been independent and autonomous bodies, though subject, as all other institutions, to the law of the land. Their constitutions are regulated by Acts of Parliament, which have, at any rate during the past century, invariably resulted from Royal Commissions of Inquiry into their affairs. But however much such commissions may have been directed towards the elimination of abuses, the principle of the academic freedom of the universities has always been regarded as inviolate. The universities have taught, or not taught, what has seemed good to them in the manner they have thought best. This principle was preserved intact, was not indeed questioned, even after 1919, when the University Grants Committee was established and the universities and colleges began to rely, in the aggregate, upon the British Treasury for up to one-third of their income, and in the case of some institutions for very much more.

It was this principle which was now felt to be at stake. As development plans were formulated, it became clear that not only would the Treasury grant have to form a much larger proportion of the universities' income, but also that the major part of the cost of capital expenditure, hitherto regarded as almost entirely a matter of universities' private resources, would have to be met from public funds.

It was generally felt that this required some readjustment in the relations between the universities and the State. In 1943 the Parliamentary and Scientific Committee, in the Report previously referred to, proposed that there should be a more thorough oversight of university development as a whole and more co-ordination in planning university work than hitherto. After long and anxious deliberation the Committee of Vice-Chancellors and Principals concurred. In a memorandum dated 6th July 1946[1] they wrote:

'. . . the Universities may properly be expected not only individually to make proper use of resources entrusted to them, but collectively to devise and execute policies calculated to serve the national interest. And in that task, both individually and collectively, they will be glad to have a greater measure of guidance from the Government than until quite recent days they have been accustomed to receive.'

They made, however, the reservation that:

'. . . the Universities should continue to be in the fullest sense self-governing societies, accountable for what they do or fail to do, properly subject to criticism, and affected in their fortunes by the public judgement of their policies, but in the last resort, their own masters.'

That position being accepted—and the Committee believed it 'to be common ground to all who have been concerned with the subject':

'The Vice-Chancellors would be glad if the University Grants Committee were formally authorized and equipped to undertake surveys of all the main fields of University activity designed to secure that as a whole the Universities are meeting the whole range of national need for higher teaching and research.'

The necessary change in the University Grants Committee's terms of references was made in the same month. The original terms of reference given to the Committee on its establishment in 1919 had been:

'To inquire into the financial needs of university education

[1] *A note on University Policy and Finance in the Decennium 1947–56*, p. 14.

in the United Kingdom and to advise the Government as to the application of any grants that may be made towards meeting them.'

The Treasury now redefined the Committee's terms of reference as follows:

'To inquire into the financial needs of university education in Great Britain; to advise the Government as to the application of any grants made by Parliament towards meeting them; to collect, examine and make available information on matters relating to university education at home and abroad; and to assist, in consultation with the universities and other bodies concerned, the preparation and execution of such plans for the development of universities as may from time to time be required in order to ensure that they are fully adequate to national needs.'

There were, naturally, some fears expressed that with the best will in the world this wide extension of the Committee's range of activity, and by implication of its powers, could not but infringe upon the treasured autonomy of the universities. These fears have, happily, so far proved to be groundless; nor was there in 1952 any more reason to dread their realization than there was in 1946. If anything, there seemed less.

In its report on the quinquennium 1947–52[1] the University Grants Committee summed up the position as follows:

'The Government have recognized that the importance of academic independence justifies a freedom from control that would not ordinarily be allowed to bodies so largely financed from public funds. It is in the continuance of this spirit of forbearance that we place our trust for the future. The prospect of its continuance seems to us to be good. The freedom which the State has left to the universities has, we believe, fostered on their side a sense of responsibility which might have withered under any attempt at control. Moreover, the dependence of

[1] *University Development.* Report on the years 1947 to 1952. H.M. Stationery Office, 1953, p. 76.

the universities on the State is balanced by a dependence of the State on the universities. Without the State, the universities cannot obtain sufficient funds to enable them to do their work; without the universities there would be no way of meeting the need for men and women adequately trained to advance knowledge and to hold positions of responsibility in government, industry and the professions. This mutual dependence is, we believe, fully realized on both sides, and has led to a sense of partnership which is full of promise for the future.'

Credit for this must go in part to the fact that since the reconstitution of the Committee in 1943 a large proportion of its members have been persons holding university posts. Tribute should be paid also to the wise and kindly leadership of Sir Walter Moberly, Chairman of the U.G.C. from 1936 to 1949, who held undeviatingly to the aim of cultivating 'an intimate and in many respects an informal relationship with those responsible for formulating and executing university policy'.[1] Nor should the contribution made by the university authorities be overlooked; it is safe to say that without exception they accepted the altered conditions in the spirit in which they were intended and have used them to further the purposes they were designed to fulfil.

For all parties concerned the task of building this new relationship between the universities and the State was, in the words of the U.G.C.,[1] 'immensely facilitated by the fact that the Government adhere, no less firmly than the universities themselves, to the fundamental principle of academic autonomy'. And it must be added, the Government's attitude was, and is, wholeheartedly supported by practically every section of responsible public opinion. That is the fundamental reason why 'the relationship between the State and the universities which is now being evolved may properly be conceived as a form of partnership'.[2]

[1] *University Development from 1935 to 1947*, p. 8.
[2] ibid., p. 82.

A not unimportant factor contributing towards the building of an harmonious relationship was the increasingly important part which the University Grants Committee played during the war in acting as a 'channel of communication between the State and the universities'.[1] Its initiation in 1943, at the request of the Committee of Vice-Chancellors and Principals, of an exhaustive examination of the universities' financial needs has already been noted. In the spring of 1944 it began to concern itself with other aspects of post-war reconstruction.

In April of that year, after consultations with the Committee of Vice-Chancellors and Principals, it sent to the Chancellor of the Exchequer a memorandum urging:

(i) the release of members of university staffs from Government departments by the autumn of 1944[2] and from the Forces at the earliest possible moment after the end of hostilities in Europe,

(ii) the return to universities of buildings occupied by Government departments by autumn 1944, or at latest directly after the end of fighting in Europe,

(iii) that a proportion of students in all subjects be allowed to enter the university straight from school, together with specified categories of men from the Forces.

In June a deputation from the U.G.C. was told that the Government could not yet take any decision, but that when it could the universities would be given high priority. In September a second deputation was given the much more cheering news that applications would be considered for the early release of members of university staffs from the civil service, that the return of buildings would be expedited, and that the release of students would be set in motion for the academic year 1945–6. Though the machinery set up for these purposes creaked in parts rather badly, the promises were fulfilled sufficiently well

[1] *ibid.*, p. 8.
[2] The memorandum was based on the assumption that the war in Europe would end in 1944 or shortly afterwards.

to enable the universities to resume normal activities on a large scale in 1945–6, with several thousand more students in attendance than they had ever had before.

Unfortunately, this meant from the start a severe overcrowding of lecture rooms, laboratories and residential facilities which grew progressively worse as student numbers increased. Even before the war the universities had been seriously short of buildings of all kinds. During the war practically all university building ceased, while, as has been noted, many buildings were destroyed or seriously damaged by enemy action. And after it shortages of man-power and materials for years restricted new building to a small fraction of the most urgent projects.

Much was done by improvisation, including the holding of classes in duplicate or even triplicate, and by taking over and adapting domestic, hotel and other premises. At Oxford and Cambridge the colleges, by 'doubling-up' their residential accommodation, that is, by putting two or more men into a set of rooms previously occupied by one, by ranging far and wide into the surrounding countryside for lodgings, and by sanctioning such unprecedented—and wholly undesirable—innovations as hutments in quadrangles and courts, managed to get by without total loss of the gracious amenities which are so essential a feature of life at the ancient universities. But the civic universities and the university colleges, which were increasing their numbers proportionately to a far greater extent,[1] were in truly desperate straits.

The U.G.C. cited in their 1947 Report[2] an instance of 'a university department accommodated in converted dwelling houses which were condemned as unfit for human habitation as long ago as the last decade of the nineteenth century'. This case was exceptional only in the reason which rendered the premises unsuitable.

---

[1] By 1947 Oxford had increased the number of its students from 5,023 (1938–9) to 7,500, Cambridge from 5,931 to 6,943.

[2] *University Development 1935–47*, p. 52.

Altogether, the U.G.C. estimated, £40,000,000 worth of new buildings ought to be erected during the quinquennium 1947–52. The then Chancellor of the Exchequer, Dr. Hugh Dalton, in 1947 indicated that he was quite prepared to finance a programme of this size, but said that owing to shortages of material and labour he thought not much more than half as much would be possible. In the event, rather under £11,000,000 worth of new building and large-scale reconstruction was accomplished by February 1952.

All things considered, even this must be reckoned remarkable; it is certainly unprecedented in the history of university building in this country. Nearly a hundred major projects were begun in England and Wales, and of these more than half were completed, or almost completed, by the end of 1951. The achievement is the more remarkable in that nearly two-thirds of the projects were buildings for the teaching of science and technology, which are considerably more difficult to build and far more difficult to equip than buildings for the teaching of the humanities.

In every discussion about university reform which has taken place during recent years the importance of a period of residence for students has been emphasized. As early as 1936 the University Grants Committee declared:[1]

'The system of halls of residence is, when effectively developed, a system of great educational value . . . It affords students exceptionally favourable opportunities for the stimulating interplay of mind with mind, for the formation of friendships, and for learning the art of understanding and living with others of outlook and temperament unlike their own. It can be, and often is, a great humanizing force.'

Before the war a number of English universities and colleges —notably Reading, Exeter, Hull, and Southampton—were making steady progress towards being fully residential. The influx of students after the war set back severely this develop-

[1] *Report on University Development, 1931–5.* H.M. Stationery Office, 1936.

ment everywhere: the proportion of resident students at Reading, for example, dropped from two-thirds to one-third. But the setback did nothing to diminish belief in the value of residence; on the contrary, it strengthened it. So much so that university authorities became convinced that the provision of additional Halls of Residence ought to be given the highest priority among building projects.

In 1947 the Committee of Vice-Chancellors and Principals set up a Commission of Inquiry, under the chairmanship of the Rector of Lincoln College, Oxford, Dr. K. A. H. Murray, to make a study of existing Halls of Residence and to make recommendations for the satisfactory planning of new halls. The Report of this commission, circulated in 1948, fully confirmed the opinions that had been formed about the educational value of Halls of Residence. But it also showed what a formidable undertaking it would be to provide residential accommodation for any large proportion of the greatly enlarged student population. It estimated the capital cost at somewhere between £1,500 and £1,800 a student place, which meant that to build sufficient halls to ensure that one-half of the student population would be in residence would cost something of the order of £50,000,000. 'Even to restore the pre-war proportion of students living in Halls', commented the U.G.C.,[1] 'would require the building of nearly 40 new Halls of 150 places each': an enterprise estimated to cost £10,000,000.

In the light of these considerations the fact that by 1952 a larger proportion of university students was in residence than in 1939 must be regarded as truly remarkable. Admittedly the increase was only about 1½ per cent, but to achieve this something over 7,000 additional places had had to be provided. Admittedly, also, only about one-sixth of these places were the result of new building; the other five-sixths had been procured by taking over and adapting hotels, private residences and military camps, some of which could hardly provide, even when

[1] *University Development, 1935–47*, p. 55.

adapted, all the amenities that could be desired. Nevertheless, it must be considered a very fine sustained effort in pursuit of a great ideal. And the fact should not be overlooked that it has enriched the universities with some of the most beautiful and well-planned Halls of Residence in the country. To particularize may perhaps be invidious, but Glen Eyre, the latest Hall of Residence for men at Southampton University, is as attractive a modern interpretation of an Oxford or Cambridge college as one could wish to see.

By the academic year 1951–2 over one-quarter (25.9 per cent) of all university students in Great Britain were residing in colleges or Halls of Residence. In England the proportion was higher: 29.2 per cent. This was largely due to Oxford and Cambridge, but it should interest others besides collectors of little-known statistics to learn that in that year five of the sixteen English university institutions had a higher proportion of students in residence than either of the two ancient universities.

The University College of North Staffordshire (of which more in a moment) had in 1950–1 152 out of 157 students in residence. The University College of Hull, which in 1949, before North Staffordshire opened, was able to claim to be the nearest to a fully residential university institution in the United Kingdom, came second with 71 per cent—653 out of 917.[1] Reading was not far behind with 64.5 per cent (664 out of 1,029). The Durham division of Durham University (which was founded as a residential institution) was slightly behind Reading at 62.3 per cent (715 out of 1,148) and slightly ahead of Exeter, which had 58.2 per cent (548 out of 942). Cambridge and Oxford, in that order, followed modestly in the sixth and seventh places with 53.9 and 51.4 per cent respectively. Of the total number of resident students in England, however, they still contributed close on 45 per cent—7,962 out of 17,908.

The University College of North Staffordshire was a radical

[1] This proportion has since been increased.

innovation, so radical indeed that its creation, in the form it took, would have been inconceivable before the war.

The Barlow Committee had recommended, as one way of easing the problem of accommodation, the founding of several new university colleges and at least one full university. But the existing universities and colleges would have none of the proposal; they were positive that by themselves they could accommodate within ten years all the undergraduate students the country needed—as indeed they proved they could—and in any case the founding of new university institutions is in this country regarded as a matter not to be taken lightly. But before the Barlow Committee reported a project had been laid before the University Grants Committee which finally disposed that body to advise one exception to a general policy of no new foundations.

Early in 1946 a group of people, chiefly hailing from the Potteries but including the then Master of Balliol College, Oxford, the late Lord Lindsay of Birker, approached the U.G.C. with a proposal for a university college of the most novel type. To counteract the prévalent over-specialization on a narrow range of studies which everyone agreed had a deleterious effect upon students, the sponsors of this project proposed that their college should give a four- instead of a three-year undergraduate course leading to a first degree. The first year, which would be compulsory for all students, was to consist of a general course covering the history of Western civilization, democratic institutions, and experimental science; and during the subsequent three years students would take shorter courses on subjects other than their specialities. As such a programme could not be fitted into the system which obtained for the securing of a London University external degree (for which all other university colleges prepared), the North Staffordshire group proposed that their projected college should be given the power to grant a B.A. degree, under the sponsorship of one or more of the established universities.

It is entirely typical of the scrupulous care invariably taken in the United Kingdom to safeguard academic standards that, although this proposal had the backing of, and was, indeed, largely inspired by, the Master of Balliol, the University Grants Committee spent two years considering whether to recommend its acceptance. It was not until February 1948 that the Committee reached the conclusion 'that an experiment on these lines would be in the interest of university education and should be encouraged'.[1] They then informed its promoters that provided they could obtain the Royal Charter necessary for the foundation of any university college, and secure for the college, as they had suggested, the sponsorship of established universities, financial aid from the Treasury would be forthcoming.

The Charter was obtained. The Universities of Oxford, Birmingham and Manchester agreed to act as sponsors, and in October 1950 the University College of North Staffordshire began its career with, as was only fitting, Lord Lindsay as its first principal. It opened, on its beautiful and spacious site of 154 acres in Keele Park near Stoke-upon-Trent, with one permanent building, several rows of hutments, a relatively young and definitely enthusiastic staff, and 147 undergraduate students. (It was unfortunate, but not disastrous, that during the busiest period of preparation the application papers for thirteen professorships were lost!)

No other new foundations were made during these years, but two well-deserved promotions occurred. In 1947 the University College of Nottingham, and in 1951 the Hartley University College of Southampton, applied to the Privy Council for the grant of a charter of incorporation as a full university. Both applications were successful, and these institutions became, in 1948 and 1952 respectively, the Universities of Nottingham and Southampton.

[1] *University Development from 1935 to 1947*, p. 10.

UNIVERSITY EXPANSION

SCHOLARSHIPS AND OTHER AWARDS

The rapid and continuous rise in the number of university students during the period under review was due in the first instance to the Further Education and Training Scheme, described in Chapter One, and later to the vastly increased number of scholarships and other awards for university education made from public funds, both central and local.

By 1947 over one-third of all university students were receiving F.E. and T. grants, and fears were being expressed that when this source of financial support dried up—as it would during the next year or two—the number of students would drop steeply. But in that year the Minister of Education, Mr. George Tomlinson, increased the number of State scholarships from 360 to 750 a year, and in April 1948 he appointed a 'Working Party' on University Awards under the chairmanship of Mr. G. G. (now Sir Griffith) Williams, a deputy secretary of the Ministry of Education, and representative of the Ministry, the universities, the local education authorities, and the teachers' associations concerned.

This Working Party was given the following terms of reference:

'On the basis of the present system of State scholarships and major awards (i.e., awards made by local education authorities) to advise on any administrative or other changes that may be desirable, particularly having regard to:

(a) the increased numbers at universities;

(b) the termination of the Further Education and Training Scheme;

(c) the probable abolition of four-year grants for intending teachers.'

The Working Party reported[1] in December 1948, recommending (*inter alia*) that:

[1] *University Awards.* H.M. Stationery Office, 1948.

'(i) Awards for university education from public funds should be of two types:
- (*a*) State scholarships, for which the Ministry of Education would be responsible;
- (*b*) Local scholarships, for which the local education authorities would be responsible.

(ii) the main purpose of State scholarships should be to assist students of high academic promise, including those holding university open scholarships or exhibitions.

(iii) Local scholarships should be available to all eligible candidates recommended and accepted by universities and university colleges and educationally qualified.

(iv) Every possible encouragement and help should be given to universities, especially London and provincial universities, to increase the number of their open scholarships and exhibitions.

(v) Four-year grants to intending teachers based on a signed undertaking (to enter the teaching profession and teach in maintained schools) should be abolished within the next three years.'

On the basis of these principles the Working Party estimated that it would be necessary to increase the number of awards for which the Ministry was responsible (i.e., State scholarships and supplementary awards) from the then figure of 2,000 to 2,500 a year to at least 4,000 a year. Of this number 2,000 should be State scholarships, and the others supplementary awards to holders of university open scholarships and exhibitions. The number of local awards, then about 4,000 a year, should be increased to a minimum of 7,000. The value of all awards should be related to parents' incomes. Below £500 a year it should be the full rate. Above that figure it should gradually diminish until a point was reached where no grant was made. The Working Party thought that this point should not be reached before an income of at least £2,000.

These recommendations were accepted by the Minister. In 1948 the number of State scholarships was raised to 800, in 1949 to 950, and in 1951 to the 2,000 proposed by the Working Party. Meanwhile the number of local awards increased proportionately; by 1950–1 the local education authorities were, in fact, considerably exceeding the minimum that had been suggested. In that year they made 10,300 awards, of which over 8,000 were major awards, that is, awards made on the standard figures of maintenance, less the specified parental contributions. As a result, by 1951–2 about 75 per cent of all full-time university students in England and Wales were receiving financial aid.

Two interesting innovations in the award of State scholarships were made in 1947: the inclusion of small numbers of scholarships open (a) to candidates under the age of 20—or exceptionally above that age—who had left school early and gone into industry, and (b) to candidates over the age of 25. The former were called Technical State scholarships, the latter State scholarships for Mature Students.

Candidates for Technical State scholarships had to have completed a course leading to an Ordinary National Certificate or Diploma, or a course of equivalent standard, and to have been in full or part-time attendance at an establishment of further education for not less than two years immediately before applying. They would therefore presumably wish to study for a scientific or technological degree, or comparable qualification. The State scholarships for Mature Students, on the other hand, were intended 'to promote opportunities for the continued study of humanistic and liberal subjects, rather than those leading to the attainment of technical or professional qualifications'.[1] From 1947 to 1950 up to a hundred Technical and twenty Mature scholarships were offered annually; in 1951 the numbers were increased to 120 and thirty respectively.

[1] Ministry of Education Administrative Memorandum No. 257, dated 3rd December 1947.

UNIVERSITY EXPANSION

Of the 120 Technical scholarships up to forty were to be reserved for candidates aged 20 or over.

A few industrial firms had for long offered university education to the occasional young employee of great promise. During the years under review the practice grew rapidly; I was told, but I cannot confirm this, that in 1949 at least 2,000 university students were being subsidized by their employers. The largest scheme was that of the National Coal Board, to which reference was made in Chapter Four. But by 1952 there were few among the front-rank industrial concerns which were not maintaining employee-students at universities.

PROBLEMS OF ALL KINDS

Throughout the war there was widespread discussion about almost every aspect of university policy and practice. Early in 1944 the National Union of Students issued a long list of points for debate; this included the relationship between the universities and the rest of the educational system, the revision of university courses and teaching methods, degree standards, and the employment of graduates. The British Association's Committee on Post-War University Education had examined most of these and other points in the series of reports it published in 1942 and 1943. In the spring of 1944 the Association of University Teachers issued a memorandum in which, in addition to urging that a year of residence for every student should be made available immediately after the war, and that a completely residential system should be aimed at, it advocated the creation of two new degree courses, one special and one general, and proposed that decisive steps be taken to raise the status of the civic universities to something approaching that of Oxford and Cambridge.

The immense influx of students after the war brought many new problems and intensified most of the old. Material problems naturally attracted the largest share of public attention; they are easy to understand, and have a habit of making themselves uncomfortably obtrusive. But underlying the questions of accommodation, staffing, salaries, maintenance grants and so on were more fundamental ones which did not escape the notice of the discerning.

Persistent throughout all these years was a profound concern, not restricted to university circles, about the quality of university work. This question is a dual one; it concerns the quality of the students entering the university and that of the staff who will teach them—not only there, it should be noted, but also beforehand in the schools. The two aspects are, of course, complementary; each directly and inevitably affects the other. Towards both university opinion, and with it all informed public opinion, maintained an unvarying attitude which was aptly epitomized in words of the Barlow Report:[1] 'Whatever happens, the quality of our university graduates must not be sacrificed to quantity.' But that is easier to say than to secure.

'Academic standards once lowered are not retrievable; and Gresham's Law applies to them', wrote the Committee of Vice-Chancellors and Principals in the memorandum on university policy and finance[2] submitted to the U.G.C. in 1946. The U.G.C. report on *University Development from 1935 to 1947* discussed the problem at some length, and while making no dogmatic judgements about it generally recorded one opinion of considerable, and some people would say dangerous, significance:

'. . . though very many students of lower grade academical attainment are well worthy of a university education, their scholastic standard is not enough, by itself and in default of other qualifications, to make their years at the university a good national investment.'[3]

By which, presumably, the Committee meant that they should not be assisted out of public funds: an argument which

[1] Para. 25, p. 8.   [2] p. 5.   [3] p. 34.

could easily lead to the establishment of two academic standards in university education, one for scholars and the other for private fee-payers.

The Committee returned to the question of the quality of students in its 1947–52 survey, where it made the following observations:[1]

'In the faculties of science and technology in which student numbers have doubled since the war, there has been only a small increase in the number of outstandingly able people. On the other hand, the really weak students who used to get into universities before the war have been unable to gain admittance. The consequence of these tendencies is that, in relation to the total number of students, the proportion of outstandingly good and outstandingly weak students is lower, and that of good second-class students higher, than it used to be. The situation in the arts faculties is not greatly different . . .'

University teachers in general, said the Committee,[2] were well satisfied with the quality of the students entering the universities; despite the effect of the war upon their early education they arrived at the university with better formal qualifications than students of former days, they applied themselves diligently to their studies, and they responded encouragingly to efforts made to interest them in other fields of knowledge.

The Working Party on University Awards, though careful to state explicitly that they were concerned 'not with major social questions . . . but with administrative and other changes in the present system of awards',[3] obviously had the question of quality in the forefront of their minds throughout their deliberations. This is quite clear from paragraph 34 of their Report, in which they suggest that a university would presumably consider applications for entry mainly on three grounds:

(i) Ability, attainments and inclinations of applicant;
(ii) Personality and character of applicant;
(iii) Degree of competition from other applicants.

[1] *op. cit.*, p. 25. [2] p. 26. [3] p. 1.

'In normal circumstances', added the Working Party,[1] 'a candidate recommended and accepted by a university, who has reached the advanced standard in two subjects in one examination for the General Certificate of Education and shown satisfactory evidence of general education, should be given an [L.E.A.] Award.' That is about as far as thought had got by 1952 on the exceedingly difficult, and perhaps insoluble, problem of the balance between academic qualifications and qualities of personality and character to be looked for in candidates who do not establish a claim to entry on grounds of intellectual ability alone.

The Working Party raised another aspect of the question which was troubling all university authorities and provoking controversy between two schools of thought. What, it asked, should be the tests for open and State awards? The Barlow Committee had asserted[2] that:

'In few other fields are numbers of so little value compared to quality properly developed. Character, temperament and wider qualities of mind are, of course, as important as intellectual acuity and the test for fitness for the universities is not intelligence alone.'

The Working Party concluded[2]—and no one really disputed this conclusion—that there were some candidates possessing 'qualifications of an academic kind which can be tested with reasonable accuracy by examination results', and who by this test gave evidence of intellectual capacity which suggested that they would obtain first or good second-class honours degrees. To these the Working Party would award Open or State scholarships without further question, though with one proviso, that 'examiners or awarding boards should have the right to call for a confidential report from the school . . . and, if the occasion justifies, to interview particular candidates'.[3] This, presumably, only in borderline cases or where there was reason to suspect temperamental instability.

[1] p. 11. [2] p. 8. [3] p. 9.

These intellectual high-flyers would, however, be but a small minority among candidates. In the 'less easily assessed' majority the Working Party distinguished two special types: those 'whose academic gifts, often of a high order, do not develop fully until they reach the university', and those who 'without showing outstanding academic ability' possess 'other talents of a high order'. It was about the admission of this second type that controversy raged.

It was not a new controversy. To go no farther back than 1943 the 'Norwood' Report on *Curriculum and Examinations in Secondary Schools* specified[1] three types of pupils 'who will go to the University': first, those of 'outstanding and exceptional intellectual ability and of scholarly mind', who will gain their places on 'sheer intellectual merit alone'; second, those of 'good intellectual ability' and wide interests, who may be expected to obtain at least a second-class honours degree and to make a valuable contribution to the general life of the university; and third:

'... the boy (or girl) who is not a natural student but is of reasonable intellectual capacity; interested in ideas, theoretical or practical, without being good at examinations; of strong personality and character, able to take the lead, and an asset to any common life.'

'Such men or women', declared the Norwood Committee, 'a University cannot afford to be without'. Other people, however, took a very different view, and some went so far as to say that the Norwood Committee had done the universities a grave disservice by advocating the admission of such students. It is of interest, and by no means surprising, to note that precisely the same controversy raged over the admission of pupils to grammar schools. In neither field has any generally agreed principle as yet been arrived at.

Another dispute, to which again no definite answer has been found, is about the proportion of people in the population who

[1] p. 36.

UNIVERSITY EXPANSION

are intellectually capable of profiting from a university education. The Barlow Committee, on the strength of test experiments conducted in Scottish universities by Professor (later Sir Godfrey) Thomson and at Manchester by Dr. Grace Leybourne-White, concluded that[1] 'only about one in five of the boys and girls who have intelligence equal to that of the best half of the university students actually reach the universities'. This led them to the further conclusion that 'there is clearly an ample reserve of intelligence in the country to allow both a doubling of the university numbers and at the same time a raising of standards'.

The Committee of Vice-Chancellors and Principals, in the 1946 memorandum previously quoted, were not so sure: 'the sufficiency of the evidence' cited, they declared,[2] 'is a matter on which the Vice-Chancellors feel that much more investigation is needed'. On the whole the history of the following five years tended to confirm the wisdom of this more cautious attitude. By 1952 there was a very general opinion that, for a while at least, the upward growth in numbers should be checked. So far as could be judged, at about 65,000 the English universities and university colleges were receiving roughly as many students of university calibre as the nation seemed able to produce. Several universities, indeed, were gravely perturbed by the proportion of students failing the examinations set at the end of the first and succeeding years. In discussing the question of total numbers it has to be remembered that between 1945 and 1952 the entry was coming from years of very low birth-rate—the mid-1930s—and that therefore numbers must be expected to increase again in the future.

Whether university standards of work were generally maintained during these years of expansion I think it as yet impossible to determine. Many people have asserted that they were not, some even going so far as to declare that they deteriorated seriously. But there is always a tendency to suggest that to-day,

[1] para. 26, p. 9. [2] p. 4.

especially if it be a day of changes, is never as good as yesterday.

I am not competent to offer any opinion on the question, which involves far more than academic attainment as tested by formal examination. If it be taken out of this narrower context the fact has to be reckoned with that during these years the universities admitted large numbers of young men and women who before the war would not even have contemplated the possibility, except perhaps as a Utopian dream, of a university career. In other words, they admitted large numbers of students who for economic reasons would have been excluded before the war, and who for these reasons lacked the social background, with all that this implies of wider interests, which could be assumed for most university students before the war. As the University Grants Committee observed in the 1947–52 report:[1]

'. . . we have no doubt that it would be the general view of the universities that a much higher proportion of their students than formerly are young men and women who have few cultural interests and attainments beyond those which they have acquired at school. The presence in the universities of relatively large numbers of students who lack the advantages of a cultured home background has forced upon the universities a number of problems of teaching and the organization of student life which were not hitherto generally recognized.'

At the same time, because of the far greater competition for places, the universities have undoubtedly excluded since the war considerable numbers of young people who while possessed, perhaps amply, of this social background have not the high level of intellectual capacity necessary now to secure entry. These changes cannot but have affected standards at the universities, and will have far-reaching repercussions upon the quality of national life. Whether these will ultimately affect it for better or worse I for one would not be prepared to say. Nor would I be sure that any such present changes will be per-

[1] p. 24.

manent. The universities, like all British institutions, have a great capacity for incorporating new elements and, while being modified by these, of moulding them gradually into a pattern which preserves the traditional virtues of university life.

One problem arising out of the changed economic and social background which perturbed many minds was that 'students are unduly preoccupied with examinations and . . . fail to use their time at universities to broaden their minds'. The University Grants Committee, in noting this common complaint,[1] expressed the fear that 'these defects may be partly attributable to courses which overpress the student and leave him with insufficient time for reading outside his curriculum'. That is undoubtedly true, especially of scientific and technological courses. But the problem goes far deeper, and is of the utmost social significance. To the poor boy, or girl, the economic possibilities held out by a university career are overwhelming; and as a rule the student's family and friends persistently harp upon them. But to realize those possibilities it is necessary to pass, and pass well, the university's examinations. To fail is the ultimate disaster. Can it be wondered at that students are 'unduly preoccupied with examinations'?

In commenting, perhaps somewhat inadequately, upon this problem the U.G.C. reminded the universities[2] that their task was not only to 'provide the specialists of to-morrow', but also to 'educate men and women capable of holding positions of responsibility in every walk of civil life'. If one puts it no more highly than that, the reminder was probably unnecessary; but surely it is the function also of the university to educate men and women towards a conception of the purpose and dignity of human life at its best? To have no higher aim than to educate them to hold 'positions of responsibility' could still leave the universities no more than high-level vocational training establishments, regarded, justly, by students as a means of obtaining superior professional qualifications.

[1] *University Development*, 1947–52, p. 45.   [2] *op. cit.*, p. 45.

All the foregoing questions and others yet more profound were brilliantly analysed in a book published in April 1949 under the perhaps somewhat too sensational title of *The Crisis in the University*.[1] Written by Sir Walter Moberly, who was at the time still Chairman of the University Grants Committee, the book was the fruit of a prolonged series of discussions by groups of university teachers and others arranged by the Student Christian Movement and the Christian Frontier Council—the latter being, as Moberly explained,[2] a 'small body of Christian laymen who endeavour to work out together the bearing of their faith on secular life to-day, particularly in the spheres of their own professional responsibilities'. In some of these discussions I was privileged to be present.

'The crisis in the university', declared Sir Walter,[3] 'reflects the crisis in the world and its pervading sense of insecurity', and he asked:[4]

'Can the universities adapt themselves to a world of insecurity? Have they anything creative to contribute to it or are they themselves immersed, or about to be immersed, in the maelstrom? Can they "rise to the height of the times"?'

In their present state, Sir Walter contended,[5] they could not, because:

'Beneath the façade of development and hopefulness, the British universities to-day share with the universities of the world a peculiar malaise and impotence. They have little inner self-confidence, because they lack, and are increasingly aware that they lack, any clear, agreed sense of direction and purpose. At this moment they cannot give an effective lead because they themselves share, and have shown small sign of transcending, the spiritual confusion of the age.'

'In particular', declared[6] Sir Walter, 'the universities are

---

[1] Published for the Christian Frontier Council by the S.C.M. Press Ltd. 1949.
[2] *The Crisis in the University*, p. 8.
[3] *ibid.*, p. 15.   [4] *ibid.*, p. 77.   [5] *ibid.*, p. 21.   [6] *ibid.*, p. 22.

not now discharging their former cultural task.' This he defined, in the words of Professor Bonamy Dobree,[1] as:

'... the creation, generation by generation in a continuous flow, of a body of men and women who share a sense of civilized values, who feel responsible for developing them, who are united by their culture, and who by the simple pressure of their existence and outlook will form and be enlightened public opinion.'

Moberly accused the universities[2] of being false to 'the ideals to which the university traditionally professes allegiance' by turning out narrow specialists instead of 'rounded persons', and of encouraging in their students a 'self-centred and utilitarian' instead of a 'liberal and disinterested' attitude to study. He said that they were failing to 'cultivate objectivity and impartiality', and degrading what ought to be a community exercising 'a transforming influence on its members' by awakening in them a sense of wonder through contact with inspiring persons into 'a bargain counter, at which certain specific articles they require are purveyed'.

Moberly went on to examine the historical conceptions of the university's task. These were successively, he said, the Christian-Hellenic, the Liberal, and the Technological and Democratic, the last being the conception now holding sway, though not unchallenged.

'We have had the Classical-Christian university, which was later displaced by the Liberal university. This in turn has been undermined, but as yet not superseded, by the combined influence of democratization and technical achievement.'[3]

'What we have, in fact, to-day', he declared, 'is the chaotic university', and he went on to analyse the causes of the present state of disintegration which he diagnosed. 'Broadly speaking', he said,[3] 'the university to-day is not asking the really fundamental questions. In particular there has been something like

[1] Article in the *Political Quarterly*, No. XV, p. 343 quoted p. 22.
[2] pp. 23–4.   [3] p. 50.

a taboo on the treatment of contentious issues of politics and religion.'

'. . . such a taboo is disastrous and indefensible. It confines university education to the use of means as opposed to the choice of ends, to training in the acquisition and handling of tools as opposed to appreciation and criticism of the larger purposes for which those tools are to be used. It abjures any contribution to answering the master-question—How shall a man live?'

To Moberly this question was the one to which above all others the university must address itself. Neutrality, posing as 'academic detachment', was an abdication of responsibility. It meant that:

'Most students go through our universities without ever having been forced to exercise their minds on the issues which are really momentous. Under the guise of academic neutrality they are subtly conditioned to unthinking acquiescence in the social and political *status quo* and in a secularism on which they have never seriously reflected.'[1]

In seeking to discover the remedy for this profoundly disturbing state of affairs, Moberly examined critically the claims of classical and scientific humanism, and of the 'back to the Christian tradition' school of thought. He found them all inadequate. Though writing as a Christian, and presenting what he conceived should be the Christian attitude towards the fundamental problems of the university, he had no doubt whatever that to attempt to use the university as an evangelizing agency for Christianity would be utterly wrong.

'First it is impracticable. Secondly, even if it were practicable, it would be inequitable. Thirdly, even if it were equitable, it would, from a truly Christian point of view, be disastrous.'[2]

Christians, he said, had to realize that they were to-day a small minority. It was therefore 'unfair and unreasonable to ask that the universities shall be dominated by Christian belief'.[3]

[1] p. 51.   [2] p. 101.   [3] p. 102.

Even if such a demand were successful it would not further the Christian cause but rather do it harm because 'the adoption of a Christian platform by the university to-day . . . would inevitably be a sham'.[1] The function of Christians in the university was to 'play the role of a "creative minority" ' which would aim at 'exercising influence on the university as a whole'.[2]

On the broad issues of the aim, the basis and the function of the university Moberly held, first, that the university 'must be a community within which the chief contemporary intellectual positions . . . may enter into a living encounter with one another'.[3] If it had to be officially neutral on ultimate issues, it must at least be positively, not negatively, neutral; that is, it should neither exclude nor discourage discussion of fundamental questions but actively promote and encourage it.

Secondly, the university should strive to re-open communication between scholars who, through adherence to different philosophies and ways of life, were no longer able to converse with each other on any serious subject. And thirdly, the university should define, commend and build its corporate life upon the basic values and virtues to which all engaged in university work would assent. Of these Moberly proposed six:

(i) . . . the conviction that the things of the mind are worth pursuing, developed to an intensity at which it becomes an intellectual passion. (p. 121.)

(ii) . . . the duty of intellectual thoroughness, of pursuing the argument wherever it may lead. (p. 122.)

(iii) . . . the obligation to be meticulously accurate in dealing with empirical evidence. (p. 123.)

(iv) . . . the obligation to approach controversial questions with the temper of the judge rather than of the advocate or the notorious 'expert witness'. (p. 124.)

(v) insistence on freedom of thought and publication (p. 125.)

(vi) . . . the conviction that the university has indeed a

[1] p. 103. [2] p. 301. [3] p. 107.

social responsibility, but that this is first and foremost a responsibility for focusing the community's intellectual conscience. (p. 126.)

The basic values for which Moberly thought the university should stand included 'the existence of "moral law" having authority',[1] 'a sense that it is right to be up and busy',[2] 'the conception of the good life as embodying the cardinal virtues of wisdom, temperance, courage and justice . . . and . . . an ingrained respect for law and order',[2] and 'respect for the individual as possessing rights and responsibilities'.[3] To these values all universities in the Western civilization should adhere. In addition, there were others for which British universities should stand, because they were 'inherent in the British way of life': these were tolerance, 'belief that a balance between continuity and change is both needful and possible', and the 'conviction that "Democracy is meaningful and right".'[4]

In succeeding chapters Moberly ranged over the entire field of university life and went beyond it to discuss the relationship between the university and the State, the local community, and other educational institutions. It is not possible in a brief summary to go into any detail about these chapters; suffice to say that there is hardly an aspect omitted nor any that is not touched with wisdom and clarity.

While the book commanded a wide measure of assent it was by no means to everyone's taste, and, as Moberly no doubt had hoped, it provoked a great deal of controversy. The most radical and persistent critic was Mr. Michael Oakeshott, who was then a Reader in Political Science at the University of Cambridge.[5] In the *Cambridge Journal* of June 1949 Mr. Oakeshott objected strongly to the note recurrent in the book of what might be described as a revivalist call to redemption, and roundly declared that the reforms in university life and studies

---

[1] p. 129.   [2] p. 130.   [3] p. 131.   [4] p. 132.
[5] In 1950 Mr. Oakeshott succeeded the late Mr. Harold Laski as Professor of Political Science at the London School of Economics.

which Moberly advocated were unnecessary and undesirable. But Mr. Oakeshott rather tended to lose himself in dialectic—as unfortunately did Sir Walter when he replied—and thus to blur the larger issues involved.

The great body of discussion, both spoken and written, which arose immediately upon publication of the book showed that it touched thoughts present in men's minds, even if these had not so far found overt expression. To attempt to cover in short space the variety of opinions voiced during the following months is impossible; one example may perhaps be given as illustrative.

In November 1949 the editor of the *Universities Quarterly*[1] devoted the entire number to a symposium of eight articles under the general heading of 'The Mission of a University'. All the articles had an eye to the issues raised in Moberly's book. In introducing the symposium the editor said[2] that there seemed to be 'pretty wide agreement' on three points:

(i) that in most universities to-day too little time and energy is being spent on individual students by a very busy teaching staff.

(ii) that far more stress is laid on the acquiring of information than used to be the case forty years ago and that their (i.e., the students') time-tables of routine commitments are very much fuller than they used to be.

(iii) that a very great deal of the 'research' which university teachers are so eager to do to-day is rather more of the character which is associated with the modern Ph.D. than the traditional D.Lit. or D.Sc.

On other, more fundamental, issues the contributors to the symposium were also agreed. None would have contested—nor indeed would any university teacher contest—Mr. Lionel Elvin's[3] assertion that:

---

[1] Turnstile Press Ltd.   [2] p. 16.
[3] Mr. Elvin was then Principal of Ruskin College, Oxford. In 1950 he became Director of the Educational Department of Unesco.

'The essential, the indispensable, academic freedom is the freedom of the teacher and the research worker to teach what they believe to be sound and to work at what they believe to be important without pressure from outside interested parties.'

All the contributors, and again all university teachers, would have agreed with Professor M. L. Oliphant's[1] definition of a university as[2] 'a corporate body of individuals whose aim is to preserve and continually review knowledge and culture gained in the past, and aggressively to attack and extend the frontiers of knowledge'. But I doubt whether all his fellow contributors would have agreed (certainly many university teachers would violently disagree) with his rider that 'the universities, including Oxford and Cambridge, have largely discarded these functions in favour of purely vocational training and investigations designed to solve *ad hoc* problems of the day, rather than to extend knowledge and scholarship'.

Nor, as was made clear in a following article, did they all share Professor Oliphant's view that 'the applied sciences, as at present taught and developed, are out of place in a university'.[3] Mr. John Adams, Warden of Crewe Hall, Sheffield University, replied that[4] 'from earliest times training for professional skills had been a characteristic function of the universities', and asked:

'Who is to say that the scientific study of materials, construction techniques, or forms of propulsion is not an important and worthy part of our culture? Is it not the duty of the university to promote such work and to provide facilities for undergraduates to enter upon it, provided that the social importance of the technology be established and that the discipline is such that the undergraduate is not given a mere technical drill, but is stimulated to think and inquire on logical scientific lines and to see the wider bearings of his study?'

---

[1] Professor Oliphant was then Director of the Department of Physics at Birmingham University; he later became Vice-Principal and Professor of Physics at the Australian National University, Canberra.

[2] pp. 19–20.   [3] p. 20.   [4] p. 64.

No generally accepted answer has yet been formulated to these questions. The place of technology in the universities is still disputed. As has been recorded in Chapter Four, in 1952 the Government rejected the proposal—to which the agreement of all the technical associations had been secured—for a Royal College of Technologists and announced its decision to establish a University of Technology. The experiment will be of the greatest interest, but it will not provide the complete answer to either the narrower question of the academic status of technology or the broader one of the place of vocational training in the university.

Both these are questions of degree rather than of kind. 'It is generally accepted', wrote the University Grants Committee in 1948,[1] 'that it is the responsibility of the universities to provide facilities for education in all the academic disciplines, for the appropriate training required by entrants to the various professions and for the promotion of fundamental research.' The problem, yet unresolved, is to find the right balance between these three functions, and to render them so complementary that they will make a single beneficial impact upon all engaged in university work, whether as students or teachers.

There can never be any final answer to the question: What is the function of the university? At least, not in a dynamic democratic society, which must necessarily believe, in Moberly's words, 'that a balance between continuity and change is both needful and possible'. In making change there will be both gains and losses, some of either temporary only, some permanent. During the eight years here passed in review there have been initiated—it is no more than that—greater and potentially more far-reaching changes in the relationship between the university and society than at any other time in the long history of the British universities. These changes have inevitably caused for the time being some blurring of the concept of the university's function and some lack of balance in

[1] *University Development between 1935 and 1947*, p. 81.

university practices. It is incontestable, for example, that many of the men and women who came to the university on F.E. and T. grants did so solely to gain a professional qualification and from no disinterested love of knowledge. Nevertheless, despite that fact, and despite the pregnant truth of Moberly's more fundamental criticisms, there is yet good reason to agree with Professor Roy Pascal's judgement[1] that 'The recent history of any university would, I am convinced, show that its growth has brought an enriching of the true university tradition.' May the forthcoming years, whether they bring further growth or a quieter period of consolidation, be found to enrich that tradition still more.

[1] *Universities Quarterly*, November 1949, p. 41.

INDEX

Adams, John, 200
Administrative Staff College, 145–6
Adult education, 47, 153–63
Aeronautics, National College of, 142–3
Age, school: see *Entry, age of;* and *Leaving age*
Agricultural education, 150–3
Alexander, Dr. W. P., v
'All-age' schools, 68, 80, 81, 87–9, 95, 148
Alnwick College, 8, 9
Anderson, Sir John, 169
Apprenticeship, 131, 133, 134
Architects' Branch of the Ministry, 49
Art departments, junior, 81, 126, 127
Ashorne Hall, 163
Ashridge, 158, 159, 161
Assistant Masters' Association, 105, 108
Attingham Park, 158
Attlee, C. R., 83

BACIE, 144
Backward children, 96, 99, 100–1
Bacon, Miss Alice, v
Barlow Committee, 170, 181, 187, 189, 191
Barrow-in-Furness, 41, 42
Bases, secondary school, 41
Belstead House, 160
Berkshire, 41
Bilateral schools, 41, 80, 117, 129
Birmingham University, 62, 63, 65, 159, 182
Birth rate, 23, 47, 48, 125
Boarding education, 37, 100
Bolton, 41
Borough Polytechnic, 142
Brighton, 41
Bristol Aeroplane Co., 50
Bristol University, 16, 62, 65, 71, 164
British Association, 166, 186
British Iron and Steel Federation, 162

British Postgraduate Medical School, 168
Brymore, 153
Building trades, 130, 134
Buildings, school: see *School buildings*
Burnham Committee, 33–5, 57, 108–11, 114
Burton Manor, 158, 160
Butler, R. A., 1, 4, 20, 30, 31, 35, 76

Cambridge Journal, 198
Cambridge University, 63, 146, 169, 170, 177, 180, 200
Cameron, Prof. R. G., 66
Central authority, co-operation with local authorities, 42
Challenge and Response, 9–14, 18
Christian Frontier Council, 194
Christianity, universities and, 196–7
City and Guilds of London Institute, 135
Coaching for grammar schools, 71–2
Coal Board, National, 135–6, 186
Code of Regulations: see *Regulations*
Co-education in medical schools, 168
Coleg y Fro, 147
Commercial schools, junior, 81, 126, 127
Common schools, 41, 77
Community centres, 47, 153, 163
Comprehensive schools, 41, 77–80, 124
Consultative Committee (Board of Education), 76
Continuation schools, 2
Cornwall, 42
County colleges, 37, 147–9
Coventry, 41, 50, 79
Croydon, 100
Cultural training, 153–63

Dalton, Dr. Hugh, 178
Darlington, 41
Day classes, 76
Day release movement, 132–5

203

INDEX

Debden House, 160
Demobilization and adult education, 154-5
Denman College, 159, 160-1
Dent, H. C., 61, 130, 164
Derby, 41
Development Group, 49
Development plans, local authorities, 1, 31, 36-45
Devon, 73-4, 103
Dillington House, 158
Diplomas in Education, 65
Direct grant schools, 81, 106-7
Divisional administration, 30-1
Dobree, Prof. B., 195
Dorset, 42
Durham, County, 39
Durham University, 62, 146-7, 180

Economies in education, vii-viii, 44, 163
Education, 74, 85
Education Act, 1918, 2, 82
Education Act, 1944 (see also under subjects throughout index), vii-viii, 1-3, 30, 44, 67
Educational Reconstruction, 77, 78
Elementary school system, 68, 69, 76, 80-2
Elvin, Lionel, 199-200
Emergency training scheme: see *Training of teachers*
Engineering trades, 133, 134
Entry, age of, 47, 48, 53
Essex, 23, 24
Estimates Committee reports, 46, 131
Evacuation, restarted in 1944, 1
Evening classes, 132-3
Examination system, 102, 116-24
'Excepted districts', 31
Exeter University College, 63, 169, 178, 180
Exhall College, 8, 58

Farm institutes, 150-2
Fee-paying system, 71, 98, 103, 110
Flemming, Sir Gilbert, 5, 58

Flemming Committee, 5, 11-12, 13, 16, 17
Flintshire, 23
Food Technology, National College of, 142
Forster, W. E., 83
Free places, 107
Further education, 130, 132, 147
    Regional advisory Councils, 136-8
    Schemes, 31, 37-8, 43, 45
Further Education and Training Scheme, 26-9, 183, 202

Gateway School, Leicester, 128
General Certificate of Education, 85, 100-2, 105, 116-24, 126, 189
Germans, residential courses for, 160, 162-3
Glen Eyre, 180
Glyn House, 147
Goldsmiths' College, 6
Goodenough Committee, 168
Governing bodies, school, 107
Grammar school teachers, 34, 105, 107-11, 112-16
Grammar schools, 67, 76, 77, 105-26
    Future development, 124-6
    Governing bodies, 107
    Selection of entrants, 70-4, 107, 190
    Statistics, 81, 119
    Transfers from and into, 103-5
    Withdrawals from, 124-6
Grantley Hall, 158, 160
Grants to local education authorities, 33
Guide to the Educational System, 78, 86

Hadow Report, 76, 97
Hambleden, Viscount, 143
Head teachers' salaries, 111-12, 114
Henderson, Sir Hubert, 83
Higher School Certificates, 116-18
Holidays, reduction, 106
Holly Royde, 159, 161
Holmes, Sir Maurice, 33
Horology, National College of,

204

INDEX

HORSA huts, 19–25, 82
Horsbrugh, Miss Florence, 122, 123, 139
Horticultural education, 150, 152
Housing estates, schools for, 45–6, 47, 79
Howland, Miss L. A., 96
Hull, 42
Hull University College, 63, 171, 178, 180
Hunter, Guy, 160, 161, 162

Independent schools, 103
Industrial Supervisors, Institute of, 145
Industry and Commerce, National Advisory Council on Education for, 137–9
Institutes of Education, 14, 55, 62–6
Intelligence testing, 72, 73–5
Isle of Wight, 41
Joint Examining Boards, 62
Journal of Education, 110

Kent, 41, 43

Labour Party, 77, 83, 124
Language teaching, 91, 92
Law Society, 121
Leathersellers' College, 142
Leaving age, raising to 15, 2, 19, 20, 30, 48, 68, 81–5, 94–5; prospective raising to 16, viii, 83, 148
Leeds University, 62, 65, 170, 171
Leicester University College, 63, 171
Leisure-time adult education, 153–63
Lewis Committee (1916), 149
Leybourne-White, Dr. Grace, 191
Liberal studies, courses of, 155
Limbrick Wood primary school, 50–1
Lindsay, K., 110
Lindsay of Birker, Lord, 181, 182
Liverpool, 39–40
Liverpool University, 63, 164, 169, 171

Livingstone, Sir Richard, 10
Local administration of education, 30–1, 36–7
Local education authorities, 35, 36–43
Local surveys, 88, 92
London County Council, 22, 33, 41, 78–9
London University, 63, 65, 99, 164–5, 169, 181, 184
Loveday Committees, 151–2
Luxmoore Committee, 150–1, 152

McNair Committee, 61, 63
Management training, 137, 144–7
Manchester University, 63, 65, 169, 182, 191
Martin, Miss Loveday, 10
Meals service, school, 33, 45, 47, 49
Medical education, 168
Middlesex, 41, 80
Milk in school service, 33
Mining industries, 134, 135–6
Minister of Education, 30, 84–5, 122
Ministry of Education, and Emergency Training Scheme, 7; flood of Circulars and Regulations (1944–5), 32–3, 35; organization, 35; criticism of, 36
Missenden Abbey, 160
Moberly, Sir Walter, 175, 194–202
Modern secondary schools, 68, 77, 80–102
    Aims, 90–1
    Biased courses, 99–100
    Building delays, 85–6
    Curriculum, 86, 91–3, 97–102
    Equipment, lack of, 85–6
    'Extra year', 88, 93–5
    Parents' attitude to, 71, 74, 101, 102
    Range of ability of pupils, 96, 98–9, 101
    Transfers from, 103–5
Montgomeryshire, 41
Multilateral schools, 41, 77–80, 124
Murray, Dr. K. A. H., 179

INDEX

National Certificates, 135, 143, 185
National Union of Students, 186
National Union of Teachers, 3, 4, 94, 109
Nation's Schools, The, 31, 78, 86
New Secondary Education, The, 89–96, 98, 120, 126, 127
Newland Park College, 9
North Staffordshire University College, 180–2
Northampton, 41
Northampton Polytechnic, 142
Northern Polytechnic, 142
Northumberland, 100
Norwood Committee, 76, 77, 116, 190
Nottingham University, 6, 62, 169, 171, 182
Nursery schools, 47

Oakeshott, Michael, 198–9
Oliphant, Prof. M. L., 200
Oliver, Prof. R. A. C., 16
Oxford University, 63, 169, 170, 177, 180, 182, 200

Parliamentary and Scientific Committee, 166, 173
Part-time education, viii, 37, 133, 148–9
Pascal, Prof. Roy, 202
Pendley Manor, 159, 160
Pensions, teachers', 33, 35
Percy Report, 136
Physical Recreation, Central Council of, 162
Plymouth, 42
Political Quarterly, 195
Populations, shifts of, 47
Portsmouth, 100
Practical subjects, education in, 92, 100
Primary schools, 32, 33, 79, 105–6
Primrose Hill, 159, 161
Private schools, 37
Professional bodies and G.C.E., 121, 122

'Project' method, 15, 87, 88, 92–3, 97–9
Public schools, 103

Raybould, Prof. S. G., 156
Reading University, 63, 171, 178, 179, 180
Recreative activities, 153–63
Reform, educational, viii, 68
Regulations, Code of, 105–6
Religious education, 32, 91
Research work, 140–1, 167, 199
Residential colleges, short-course, 157–62
Residential training centres, 162–3
Responsible Bodies, 155
Rotherham, 41
Royal Aeronautical Society, 121
Royal College of Art, 143–4
Royal College of Technologists, 139, 201
Royal Institute of British Architects, 23
Rubber Technology, National College of, 142

St. Helens, 41
Salaries, 33–5, 57, 105–14
    Area pool, 113–14
    Responsibility allowances, 113–14
Salford, 42
Scholarships, 33, 183–6
School buildings, inadequacy, 2; emergency building scheme, 19–24; progress, 36; 'operational programme' for building permanent schools, 45–7; delays in building, 45–6; 'short-term programme 1947–8', 47–8; acceleration of procedure for approving plans, 48–9; Ministry builds prototype schools, 49–52; 1,000 schools constructed, 52; priorities, 148–9 Huts, 19–24, 45–6

INDEX

School buildings (continued):
  Regulations prescribing standards, 32–3
  Restrictions on building, 23, 79, 80
School Certificates, 116–19, 122, 126
School furniture, 19, 24–5
School leaving age: see *Leaving age*
School places, 19, 23
School population, 48, 79, 80–1
School year, 106
Schoolmaster, 94, 96
Science teachers, shortage of, 114–16
Scientific manpower, 166, 170, 171
Secondary education, extension to all children, 67–70, 80–1; tripartite organization, 40–1, 75–80; transfer age, 74–5
Secondary School Examinations Council, 76, 116, 118, 119, 122–3
Secondary schools, government, 32; conduct regulations, 33; types, 75–80; Code of Regulations, 105–6
Secondary selection, 70–5
Secondary teachers, 86, 93
Secretaries, Chartered Institute of, 121
Services, education in the, 154
SFORSA furniture, 19, 24–5
Sheffield University, 63, 171
Smethwick, 40
Somerset, 23, 152–3
Southampton, 100
Southampton University, 62, 64, 169, 171, 178, 180, 182
Southend-on-Sea, 74, 103
Special places, 70, 110
Spens Committee, 76, 78
State Scholarships, 138, 183–6, 189
Stoke House, 159, 161
Stoke-on-Trent, 42
Student Christian Movement, 194
Superannuation, teachers': see *Teachers*
Swansea, 41, 79

Teachers:
  'Assessment' or examination, 16–17
  Attitude to secondary education for all, 69
  Courses for, 65
  Emergency-trained, 18–19, 82
  Graduate, 115–16
  Recruitment, 2–3, 5, 53, 55–7
  Shortage, 2–3
  Status, 57
  Superannuation, 33, 35
  'Temporary', 57, 58
  Training: see *Training*
  Uncertificated, elimination of, 57–61
Teachers from the Forces, 6
Technical colleges, 130–44
Technical education, report on, 131
Technical high schools, 76
Technical schools, junior, 76, 81, 126, 127
Technical secondary schools, 76, 77, 81, 104–5, 126–9
Technological education, 136–44, 170, 200–1
Technology, National Schools of, 141–4
Technology, University of, 139, 201
Thomson, Sir Godfrey, 191
Times Educational Supplement, 42, 72, 73, 94
Tomlinson, George, 84–5, 122, 147, 183
Training of teachers, 2–3, 53–61
  Area organizations, 62–6
  Circular (1652), 5
  Departmental Committee (1925), 13
  Emergency Training Scheme, 3–19, 53
  Grants, 6, 53–4, 59, 183, 184
  Number of students, 55
  Organization reforms, 61–6
  Universities and, 61–6
Training Colleges:
  Emergency, 5–6, 7–9, 12–13, 18, 45, 55

207

INDEX

Training Colleges (continued):
    Establishment of new colleges, 54
    Grants, 53–5
    Qualifications for entry, 121–5
Transfer between schools, 88, 103
Transport to school, 37
Trent Park College, 9, 18
Truscot, Bruce, 171–2
Tutorial classes, 155–7

Union of Lancashire and Cheshire Institutes, 135
Universities, 164–82, 186–202
    Accommodation difficulties, 176, 177
    Building programme, 178
    Employee-students, subsidized, 186
    Functions, 200–1
    Fundamental problems, 194–202
    G.C.E. and entrance, 120
    Halls of Residence, 178–80, 186
    New foundations, policy towards, 181–2
    Quality and intelligence of students, 187–91
    Staffs, 176
    Standards of work, 187, 191–3
    State, relationship with the, 172–6
    Students' preoccupation with examinations, 193
    Technical colleges, relationship with, 138–9
Universities Quarterly, 199–200
University awards, 183–6, 188–9
University education, 164–82; position in 1944, 164–5; post-war expansion, 165–72, 176–7; committee on, 166
University extra-mural departments, 155, 156
University grants, 166–70, 172–9
University Grants Committee, 138, 167–70, 172–9, 181, 182, 187, 192–3, 201

University Teachers' Association, 166, 186
Urchfont Manor, 160
Urwick Committee, 144

Vernon, Prof. P. E., 72
Vice-Chancellors and Principals, Committee of, 120, 167, 173, 176, 179, 187, 191
Village schools, closing of, 42
Vocational training, 130–47, 201
Voluntary schools, 11, 21, 43

Wales, University of, 63
Wall Hall College, 8
Wedgwood Memorial College, 159
Weeks, Sir R., 137
Welsh Department of the Ministry, 35
West Bromwich, 40
Westham House, 159, 160
Westmorland, 39, 41
Wilkinson, Miss Ellen, 20, 24, 42–3, 82, 84, 89
Williams, Sir Griffith, 183
Wilton Park, 162–3
Wokingham secondary school, 51–2
Wolfenden, J. F., 71
Wolverhampton Technical College, 142
Women students, 164, 165, 168
Women teachers, 53, 55, 58
Women's Institutes, 159, 161
Woolley Hall, 160
Workers' Educational Association, 155–6, 159
Works, Ministry of, 20–1, 24, 25
Wynyard Hall College, 9

Yorkshire, East Riding, 41
Yorkshire, North Riding, 40, 41
Y.M.C.A., 146–7, 162
Y.W.C.A., 162
Youth clubs, 47
Youth leaders, 61
Youth's Opportunity, 147

For Product Safety Concerns and Information please contact our EU
representative GPSR@taylorandfrancis.com
Taylor & Francis Verlag GmbH, Kaufingerstraße 24, 80331 München, Germany

www.ingramcontent.com/pod-product-compliance
Lightning Source LLC
Chambersburg PA
CBHW051643230426
43669CB00013B/2413